I0179303

Jamaica as it is, 1903
By
B. Pullen-Burry

PUBLISHED BY: 2024 by BTB Publishing

No part of this publication may be reproduced or transmitted in any form or by any means electronic or mechanical, including information storage and retrieval systems without permission in writing from the publisher, except for student research using the appropriate citations.

ISBN : 978-1-63652-359-0

JAMAICA AS IT IS, 1903

B. PULLEN-BURRY

"There are two oriflammes; which shall we plant on the furthest islands?—the one that floats in heavenly fire, or that which hangs heavy with foul tissue of terrestrial gold?"

—R<small>USKIN</small>.

PREFACE

In presenting this work to the British public it is proposed to bring before the notice of those unacquainted with the charms of tropical scenery some of the features which tend to make one of our oldest colonies, Jamaica, a delightful winter resort.

At present, it is visited mostly by Americans, because of its easy accessibility from New York, Boston, and Philadelphia. Their unanimous verdict is that there is no lovelier spot under the sun than this gem of the Antilles set in the midst of the waters of the Caribbean Sea.

The historical interest is sufficient to attract the student, while the artistic sense is constantly charmed by the exquisite colouring of the tropical seas, the delicious green of the waving cane-fields, the lofty mountains with their ofttimes mist-wreathed summits.

The illustrations of island scenery are by Dr Witney of East Street, Kingston, Jamaica.

In compiling this book the writer is indebted to the courtesy of Mr Frank Cundall, who placed the old histories of the colony, which are kept in the Jamaica Institute, at her disposal; also to the Archbishop of the West Indies for the information His Grace was good enough to give her, concerning the Disestablishment of the Church of England in Jamaica.

B. PULLEN-BURRY.

CONTENTS

CHAPTER I
Mandeville—Jamaica Not Near The Volcanoes—Books On The West Indies..................1

CHAPTER II
The Direct Line—The Laziness Of The Negro—Fellow-Passengers On The Port Antonio..................7

CHAPTER III
The Keswick Delegates—Miss Sarah Walker—Haytian Cannibalism..................15

CHAPTER IV
The Black Under British Rule—The Governor Of Jamaica And Suite..................25

CHAPTER V
Land Swallows—Turks Islands—An Earthquake Shock—Constant Spring Hotel..................31

CHAPTER VI
Suitable Clothing—Pedestrians In Jamaica—Self-Help Society..................45

CHAPTER VII
Dominica's Flourishing Condition—Scotch Dinner—Tropical Vegetation..................55

CHAPTER VIII
Savings Banks—Keswick Views—Spanish Town..................63

CHAPTER IX
The Royal Mail Company—The "Mumpish Melancholy" Of Jamaica 73

CHAPTER X
The Cuisine Of The E——.—The Roman Catholic Bishop Of Dominica 81

CHAPTER XI
Dr Gray On Yellow Fever—Mont Pelée—The Red Caribs Of Dominica 89

CHAPTER XII
Drives And Country Life At Mandeville—Negroes And Funeral Customs 99

CHAPTER XIII
My Visit To A Pen—Arawak Remains—Legend Of The Cotton-Tree 113

CHAPTER XIV
Obeahism And Coffee-Planting 123

CHAPTER XV
Cockpit Country—The Maroons 135

CHAPTER XVI
Indian Cattle At Montpelier—Palmer Monument In Montego Bay Parish Church—Americans 151

CHAPTER XVII
Description Of Rose Hall—Sugar—The Expense Of Working An Estate A Century Ago—Banana Cultivation 161

CHAPTER XVIII
Moneague Hotel—The Troubles Of Christopher Columbus 171

CHAPTER XIX
Women's Rights In Jamaica—A Breakdown Of The
Railway—Port Antonio—Chester Vale 181

CHAPTER XX
The Church Of England In Jamaica—Its Disestablishment,
Its Increased Activity And Development 191

CHAPTER XXI
Sir Henry Morgan—Lord Rodney—Education In
Jamaica—Captain Baker On The Bright Prospects Of
Jamaica 207

CHAPTER I

MANDEVILLE—JAMAICA NOT NEAR THE VOLCANOES—BOOKS ON THE WEST INDIES

Mandeville, *1st January 1903.*—"Our horizon is not limited by the things of time. The expectation we entertain of a future life tends to make us view things in their true proportion."

These sentences were uttered last Sunday morning by the Assistant-Bishop of Jamaica at the Parish Church of the little inland town of Mandeville, of which he is also Rector.

The occasion which called forth his eloquent sermon upon the future life was the death of Dr Temple, the late Archbishop of Canterbury.

The choice and scholarly English spoken by the Bishop, together with the breadth of thought which characterised his views, riveted my attention. Looking round at the mixed congregation of whites and blacks, I noted that the preacher had equally gained the attention of the dusky worshippers.

I wondered how much they understood of what he said, and what they really looked for in the life to come, for the creed must be simple if these grown-up children are to learn and digest it. I am told that a place where golden crowns will be placed upon their heads, harps in their hands, if they behave properly, appeals to their imagination, as do white robes to their sense of what constitutes decorous clothing for so great an occasion. One can also imagine that the old-fashioned doctrine of hell-fire would not be without efficacy as a check upon the habits of the black when he inclines to revert to his former type.

Although the negro is naturally argumentative and litigious, it will be many years before his brain adapts itself to the study of the deep things of theological casuistry.

One could scarcely expect him to grapple with the subtleties of the thirty-nine Articles, or, as I have irreverently heard them called, "the forty stripes save one," in his present evolutionary state of development.

My lot having fallen to me in a house overrun with Americans, the dignified language of that morning's sermon, and the sonorous tones of the preacher, had come as balm to my afflicted ears.

If the virility, energy, and business capacities of our friends across the Atlantic are of world-wide fame, so, honesty compels me to say, are their bragging and their boasting. When one is the only Briton amongst a crowd of Yankees, the discordant nasal voices in which they discuss food and dollars from morning till night is apt to get on one's nerves.

However, I did not come to Jamaica to write about Americans. I am glad they visit this island in search of health, and bring their much-prized dollars with them for the good of the Commonwealth.

Two months have scarcely passed since I left my native shores. Hosts of new experiences, fresh sensations and interests have filled up the intervening weeks.

I had intended to write a diary; instead, I have made some progress down that path which is said to be paved with good intentions. They say of the natives of these latitudes that "they were born tired, grew up tired, and have been tired ever since." I cannot truthfully say that of myself, although the enervating climate tries the strongest when they feel tropical heat for the first time. Energies which were rampant in the temperate zone find the end of their tether very soon under Jamaican skies. Perhaps this is why the island is said to be beneficial to persons suffering from overdone nerves. They must rest in the middle of the day; the heat is too great for any real exertion. I have not had much time to take notes, but as I propose staying four weeks in this quiet spot, I intend to gather together the mental fragments at present lying scattered about in that organ, which, for want of better knowledge, I designate my brain-pan, and piece them together into something which may be of use to people contemplating a visit to Jamaica. And I cannot help thinking if it were more generally known in England how easy it is to take such a trip, and how much there is to reward one for the trouble, many persons would be only too desirous of becoming acquainted with this lovely island.

When I told friends that I intended to visit Jamaica this winter I was amused at the hazy notion prevailing, even amongst the well-educated, not only as to its geographical position, but regarding life in general as it is lived out here.

One lady said to me, "I call it flying in the face of Providence to go so near those horrid volcanoes." I meekly explained that Jamaica lay several hundred miles away, but she went on to say, "Well! I read in the papers the other day that an American geologist says that the Pelée catastrophe is only the beginning of the end. Sooner or later all the West Indies will go."

There is no doubt that this feeling exists in some circles in England, and I think the sooner accurate knowledge replaces panic-stricken ignorance the better will it be for the colonists here, and for English people obliged to escape from the rigours of a northern winter.

It is well to know what to see in this part of the world. Several persons have said to me, both in England and in Jamaica, that they could find no guide-book to tell them how to set about taking the trip to the West Indies. I felt this want myself, and enquired at Cook's office if Herr Bædecker had found his way out here yet. He has not. Nor do I mean to forestall that conscientious and most useful Teuton. Still less do I intend to write a guide-book to Jamaica. All I propose doing is to enlighten intending visitors to these parts as to the best things to see. Very probably the greater part of them will belong to my sex. If they can have patience as I chat about persons, and tell my own experiences in my own way, they may learn things which may prove useful.

So far, I am charmed with the glorious vegetation of the tropics. There are places in this island more enchanting than any descriptions of fairyland ever penned.

Professor Haddon of Cambridge had told me before leaving England that the three most beautiful islands in the world were Java, Ceylon, and Jamaica. Having never been to the east, or nearer the tropics on land than Assouan in Egypt in the northern hemisphere, and Auckland in New Zealand in the southern, my first sight of the exuberance and prolific growth of tropical flora was like the opening of a new and attractive three-volume novel.

I am still at the first volume, and I shall only get to the end of the third when I have explored some of the Blue Mountain scenery, which, being admittedly the best thing in Jamaica, I am, in the spirit of the schoolboy who is promised cake after bread and butter, leaving to the last.

There is one small guide-book to the island which I have found out here, written by an American. It is entitled "Side Trips in Jamaica," by Mary F. Bradford, Boston and New York, Sherwood Publishing Company, and is already in its third edition. The booklet certainly carries out the object for which it was compiled, namely, to supply the need of a practical guide for tourists. There are a series of trips given for those making only a short tour, and a brief account of the historical and physical features of the island, its agriculture and government. But what is even more useful, it contains reliable information regarding trains, hotels, boarding-houses, distances, and expenses in general.

The books most generally read by visitors to these islands are Kingsley's "At Last," and Froude's "West Indies," but people find them disappointing, and say the former greatly overrated the islands. Of course, unless one is a naturalist, or, as the Americans designate that calling, a "bug-hunter," one can scarcely share the ecstasies of an expert in that branch of science. Again in these days of universal travel we cannot all visit at Government Houses, and have horses and carriages placed at our disposal. Here, one is more or less dependent upon one's own efforts, for there have not been sufficient tourists to these islands to establish any system of coaches, and one must hire one's own buggy and horse. Moreover, since the West Indies have fallen upon evil times, one hesitates before accepting proffered hospitality. Years ago things were not so; travellers were few and far between, the prosperity of the sugar-planter was proverbial, but the old order has changed owing to the decline of the sugar trade. The spirit may be, and is indeed willing, but the purse-strings are limited.

B. Pullen-Burry

CHAPTER II

THE DIRECT LINE—THE LAZINESS OF THE NEGRO—FELLOW-PASSENGERS ON THE PORT ANTONIO

I have found during my short stay in Jamaica that it is not wise to pin too much faith to the gospel of the West Indies, according to J. A. Froude, nor is it discreet to quote it to the inhabitants thereof. His book was published in 1888, and the conclusions he arrived at upon colonial problems are called Froudisms. The moral is that there is another side to West Indian questions than that of government officialism, and that these two do not hunt in couples is apparent to the most casual observer.

I must, however, refrain from discussing the subject since I intend to devote this chapter to other topics. Having yielded to the conviction that it was my bounden duty to enlighten people at home as to the easy accessibility of Jamaica, as well as to inform them what they lose by not putting in six weeks at least of one winter in this charming island, for nowhere can one see tropical scenery better than in Jamaica, I pass on to tell them the best way to get here. This they can do most directly by the Elder, Dempster steamers, which run fortnightly between Avonmouth Dock, near Bristol, and Kingston, the chief town in Jamaica. Formerly the Royal Mail Service had the monopoly of the West Indian trade, but within the last two years Mr Chamberlain has arranged with the firm of Elder, Dempster to carry the mails directly to Jamaica, which is the largest of our island possessions in these waters. These ships are called the Fruit Boats, for they return with cargoes of bananas. I believe by contract they have to bring from Jamaica 25,000 bunches every fortnight. This is the reason of the recent cheapness of this particular fruit; one may often see them on costermongers' barrows in London and elsewhere sold for a halfpenny each.

I left Avonmouth Dock 8th November 1902, in the *Port Antonio*, and a very comfortable ship I found her. Having paid a little extra, I was fortunate enough to secure a deck cabin to myself; this is quite worth the money, especially when one is approaching Jamaica. My first-class return ticket available for nine months cost £40, but there were good first-class cabins at £32. Very good stewardesses are carried on all these ships. Now the Royal Mail steamers go first to Barbadoes; at present, on account of an outbreak of small-pox last autumn, they go to Trinidad. Here they trans-ship passengers, cargo, and mails for the Leeward and Windward Islands into small inter-colonial steamers which ply between the islands, after which they proceed to Jamaica.

One avoids all this by taking the direct steamers, and, as I have said before, this island is more accessible than any I have so far visited. There are capital roads, good conveyances, and good saddle-horses, a central railway connecting the most important towns. In winter the climate is perfection, whereas nobody mentions Trinidad but to groan over their experience of the moist heat and the incessant tropical rain which makes travelling about that island too fatiguing for words, to say nothing of the risk of getting fever by not being able always to change your drenched clothing. Nor do any of the islands between Trinidad and the

Danish island of St Thomas, which I have visited, possess facilities for tourist accommodation. In some of them roads practically do not exist beyond the outskirts of the little town where the mail steamers land passengers. If horses are wanted they have to be hired from the inhabitants. The hotels, such as they are, and still more, the food, one would hardly care to take the responsibility of recommending.

It was raining as I said good-bye to my friends on the *Port Antonio*, a steamer of about four thousand tons. In fact, for some three days previously a depression had been announced, and everybody prophesied we should come in for stormy weather. We could not have had worse. It was under lowering skies and heavy rain we steamed down the Bristol Channel. The next day, Sunday, scarcely a lady moved from her berth, and most of the men appeared only to show themselves, returning again to seek the privacy of their cabins. We rolled and pitched for seven consecutive days; it was not until we had been more than a week at sea that everybody sat down to meals. Fortunately I am a good sailor, but I never boast of my prowess in that respect, knowing, to my cost, that pride goes before a fall! Some years ago I went to New Zealand by the Cape of Good Hope, and returned by the Horn, thus circumnavigating the globe. I learnt to drink cocktails off Tierra del Fuego, came in for fever and fighting at Rio, and enlarged my stock of unparliamentary language at the Canaries, where we were not allowed to land, and, instead, had to endure the slow tortures of coaling. During the whole of that voyage I suffered the discomforts of sea-sickness exactly twenty minutes, the scene of my unhappy, though transitory illness being off Plymouth, as we steamed down channel. In a moment of unguarded weakness, some months after, I boasted of this to a desponding group of fellow-passengers. We were leaving Algiers, and the sea was as smooth as it could be, but it was in the days of my innocence. I know *now* what is to be expected of the Mediterranean, and by a cruel experience I also know what a gale in the Gulf of Lions means. On my arrival at Marseilles, I had broken all previous records, and for hours had endured the pains of the condemnable. My appearance was such that my fellow-passengers forbore to taunt me with my vain boasting of the day previous. How were the mighty fallen! "All the world wondered," though they preserved a discreet and kindly silence.

Notwithstanding the rough weather we experienced in the "roaring forties," I managed to obtain a good deal of amusement and some useful information during those days of discomfort. No less famous a writer than Plato says that to travel profitably one should be between fifty and sixty. I can scarcely lay claim to as many years, still, if the chief object in going abroad be, as Plato thinks, to converse with inspired men whom Providence scatters about the globe, and from whom alone wisdom can be learnt, I hope I have succeeded in gleaning some of that golden harvest which falls before the sickle of curious enquiry. We had several interesting people on board, and whiled away otherwise tedious hours by exchanging and comparing notes of lands we had or had not travelled in.

A retired colonel, whose chief aim in life was to return to Jamaica where he had seen twenty years of service, and grow pines for the English market, assured me quite gravely he had taken up the calling of a greengrocer. On further enquiry I learnt that he was enthusiastic about the future possibilities of fruit culture, and, said he, "when we get the steamers promised us by Elder, Dempster, which are to take only ten days between Kingston and Bristol, what a chance it will be for us pine-growers!" I met this gentleman five days after landing at Kingston, at a garden-party at King's House. I thought he looked tired, and he explained that he had been working hard himself ever since he landed, planting his precious pines. I asked if he could not trust them to his gardener. "No," said he; "the blacks are very good fellows, but if you tell them to put first a layer of sand and then manure, they are bound to do the opposite. It is easier to plant them yourself." In saying this he just touched upon the sore spot in Jamaica, as I afterwards learnt. The labour question may be bad in England, but it is a very different thing in this island. Captain C——, of the Royal Mail Service, said to me one day, "We never overlook a fault amongst our black firemen; with a white man we can do so, for he will thank his stars the omission was not noticed, and will be careful not to repeat his fault, but the blacks have not sense enough for that, and we fine them one or two days' pay, as the case may be." An English lady, who had seen better days at home and has opened a boarding-house at Mandeville, said to me: "In England I used to say that I worked like a nigger. Now I say I work like an Englishwoman." The laziness of the negro is proverbial in the West Indies, yet occasionally he makes a good servant. On another occasion I was told by an old gentleman that he had often watched hard-working coolies cultivating their little patch of garden. From a window looking out in an opposite direction he had seen lazy niggers asleep all day under trees. At night, when the coolies had departed, he had watched woolly heads creep along the low fence, and steal yams and anything they could lay their hands upon, which the industrious Hindoo had planted. At the same time, I am told on unquestionable authority that when sure of good treatment, the negroes on some estates are hard-working and reliable.

In most cases the West Indian black finds the labour of three days sufficient to keep him for a week, thus the property owners soon after the days of emancipation suffered greatly from the lack of labour. To supply this want the Government imported coolies from India, and it is interesting to compare the lithe, sinewy Hindoos with their intelligent dark eyes and black straight hair with the ofttimes lumbering gait of the woolly-haired, thick-lipped sons of Ham.

One of our most popular passengers was an American lady who had seen many lands, and last, but not least, had travelled from Japan *viâ* Vladivostock and the Russian Railway down to Pekin. She had been a guest at the headquarters of each of the allied forces, and it was interesting to hear her recount her adventures. She had, she said, met with unfailing courtesy from the Russian officials, and was loud in her praises of that nation. She declared that our Indian troops had been generally admitted to be the finest body of men in Pekin. "You English," she said, "think a deal of your alliance with the Japs, but I guess that if it was to their advantage they would leave you in the lurch any day." This enterprising lady had visited the royal palace, and had photographed her Imperial Majesty of China's bed, together with other celestial furniture never before exposed to the impious gaze of foreign devils! Indeed she was a most entertaining person, and apparently had done everything there was to be done, as known to this generation.

One of our officers had been in Constantinople at the time of the Armenian atrocities. He had his tale to tell, and after one had heard from an eye-witness of the unspeakable cruelty of the Turk, but also of the utter unworthiness of the Armenian—who seems to have been as much of a *mauvais sujet* of the Porte as the Fenian was to us in years gone past—one felt glad that British blood had not been spilt in defence of so miserable a people as the Armenians. There were several persons who came out to Jamaica returning by the same steamer, and spending the four or five days in a hasty survey of the island. One couple were going on to Mexico and California. A Russian journalist, commissioned to send home articles upon Jamaica, and a majestic and venerable dame, known as the fair Delicia, were also fellow-passengers. The last-named lady is well known in fashionable circles of Kingston society. She is not far removed from that limit which is supposed to represent the average lease of life. Her amiability is not excessive, but her skittishness is phenomenal. She dances on all possible occasions, and waltzes generally with the youngest men present. She has a playful way of boasting that she cannot remember the persons with whom she has quarrelled, and reputations are at a discount when the fair Delicia engages in conversation.

B. Pullen-Burry

CHAPTER III

THE KESWICK DELEGATES— MISS SARAH WALKER— HAYTIAN CANNIBALISM

There were two persons, however, whose arrival by the *Port Antonio* was looked for with feelings of great expectation by a certain class of people living in this island, and whose ministrations, I fancy, have since resulted in airing certain questions which perhaps required to see daylight. These were two delegates from the Keswick Conference. The latter, I believe, is a yearly gathering of Evangelicals at home, and is attended by nonconformists and a certain section of Low Churchmen. Possibly the preaching which one identifies with this particular school of thought, though it is not one which appeals to me, may be adapted to the black and coloured people who attend the numerous dissenting chapels which are to be found all over the West Indies. Indeed the negro is naturally pious, or, to put it in plain English, superstitious. I believe Professor Huxley has shown that this is invariably the case with savage or undeveloped races. Be it as it may, I am quite willing to concede that whatever agency has been at work to influence these people, who two or three centuries ago were offering up human sacrifices and practising the most hideous and revolting rites in the backwoods of West Africa, to say nothing of their semi-savagery when emancipated in 1834, has been a powerful influence for good. The negro is stupid, but his evolution is going on apace compared with the slow development of many races.

The court-house of Mandeville is visible from my window, and to-day the petty cases of a large surrounding district are being tried. I have enquired what are the offences which generally come before the magistrates on these occasions. I was told from trustworthy sources that murder is most rare amongst the blacks, the cases tried being mostly petty larceny, property, or commercial disputes. Local squabbles are often settled by a clergyman, or dissenting minister, before being brought into court.

I asked if there were many cases of matrimonial ill-treatment or quarrelling, and was met by the reply, "They don't marry here." Unfortunately this is largely a fact, and constitutes a great blemish on the character of the Jamaican black. When one hears, however, the question discussed, one can hardly blame a hard-working negro woman (and most of them are that) for refusing to marry if the practical result of marriage, as it affects her, is that sooner or later she will have to keep her husband as well as her children.

Persons who have had experience with these women tell me that the instinct of maternity is the strongest they have—to them childlessness is a reproach. When they do marry they are generally faithful, but the lot which a black woman dreads more than any other is that of being a deserted wife. "Me get tired of him, sah, and he get tired of me," is a very natural excuse when the parson endeavours to legalise the bond. We know such things as husbands and wives getting tired of each other occur in our own land; the negress voices what many a white woman feels. In considering this subject—for, like the poor, it is ever with you in these parts—one must bear in mind that in slavery times the blacks were herded together like cattle on the estates. Enthusiastic reformers forget that it may take generations to eradicate their hereditary promiscuity of life.

Nobody who sees these women stride along, often walking twenty miles to the nearest market town, with baskets on their heads weighing occasionally upwards of a hundred pounds, could think them lazy, especially when one knows how poor are the weekly returns for their merchandise, which consists chiefly of home-grown yams, sweet potatoes, oranges and bananas.

An American told me he was going to Kingston by the electric tram. Beside him sat a well-dressed negro, wearing a silver watch and chain. A black woman, carrying an enormous basket heavily filled on her head, ran alongside the tram, which had slowed down. The two were talking, the man from the tram, she from the road.

"Is that your wife?" he asked the man in surprise.

"Yes, sah! dat my wife, sah," replied he.

"You lazy fellow, you ought to be ashamed of yourself!" exclaimed the American indignantly. "Why don't you let your wife ride and you walk?" he further blurted out.

"Please, sah, the women, sah, 'bout here be so kind, sah!" apologetically explained the negro in an injured voice.

This episode sufficiently illustrates the conditions of the division of labour amongst a large proportion of the emancipated Jamaican population. The Moravians have large settlements in the island as well as other dissenting bodies; but where all work together for the spiritual good of the race whom Providence has permitted to flourish and multiply in these islands it would be a work of supererogation for me to criticise their methods.

Speaking from the point of view of a fellow-passenger, one of the delegates sent out by the Keswick Convention was an interesting personality. His writings and undenominational services in South London are, I am told, well-known in nonconformist circles.

He is a tall, white-haired, venerable-looking man, and when I first caught sight of his face at Avonmouth Dock, I was forcibly reminded of a picture of the Pastor Oberlin who figured in one of my favourite story-books, when, as children, we had certain literature set apart for Sundays, other for week-days. I had several conversations with him, and I thought him to be both liberal-minded and sympathetic. He seemed to hold that the most important thing in life was not so much what one believed as what one did.

It was interesting to hear this evangelistic missioner tell how he had been brought up in the straightest and strictest school of thought, and how he had himself preached and held the most rigid doctrines as to who were to be saved and who were to be eternally damned. But travel, he said, had opened his eyes, and he now saw things from a far wider standpoint. It appears he had held many conversations with advanced and cultivated Hindoos, and he could not bring himself to believe that such beautiful souls and such refined intelligences could be doomed for ever, because they could not accept gospel truths. Personally, I have never been troubled by the teachings of such a harsh creed, but I can imagine the trial it must have been to a man of firm convictions to sever himself for ever from life-long beliefs, which, no doubt, he had preached and expounded time after time. He told me that he was going to hold meetings in different parts of Jamaica for a month. I have since read in the island papers that his sermons have been of the revivalistic order, and that the meetings have been well attended. His colleague, a clergyman of the Church of England, was by no means a *persona grata* on board ship. His religious views belonged to that exclusive and narrow school of thought in the Church of England, which happily does not find many adherents nowadays. In an extract from a sermon which he preached at Kingston, some weeks after his arrival, I read that he lamented how few people there were who would be saved! In these days of latitudinarianism and toleration there is no reason why peculiarly constituted temperaments should not cling to obsolete and effete doctrines if they like them, but it seems to me, whatever our creed may be, and however much we wish to benefit our fellows, without exercising tact, we shall do more harm than good.

This delegate from Keswick evidently thought his fellow-passengers were in a bad way, for he offered uninviting-looking religious literature to those who conversed with him; but an amusing incident in which he was chief actor quite enlivened the tediousness of the voyage. The charming American lady, of whom I have already spoken, was invited into the smoking-room one stormy afternoon by two gentlemen in order to tell their fortunes by means of palmistry. Probably this zealous clergyman had already mentally decided that she was a brand to be snatched from the burning. Although a non-smoker he confronted her, and with Hibernian eloquence harangued her as to the impropriety of her conduct in entering those precincts sacred to the cult of tobacco. It would perhaps be wiser to draw a veil over the sequel to his somewhat precipitate and uncalled-for interference. Needless to say, his own sex resented it in words which I decline to insert in these pages. At the same time one feels that it would be beneficial and a distinct gain to society at large if some of the well-meaning but indiscreet upholders of exclusive cults would consider the feelings of others and behave to those whose path crosses their own with, at least, that generous toleration and spontaneous kind-heartedness which characterises well-bred men and women of the world. The influence of a high-minded, genial Englishman who is too proud to stoop to meanness of any description, but who does not shun his fellows because their moral status is not up to his own level, is far greater than that of the narrow-minded but "superior" religionist who looks down upon a sinful generation from the pedestal of an assured salvation. It may be that the latter stands ready to reach out a hand to help up his less favoured brethren, that is, from his own standpoint, but often the out-stretched hand is a rough one, the face bending down towards the sinner is uninviting in its cold, harsh expression, and the soul that might have been helped plunges back into the strife of the waters of worldliness preferring them to a joyless, uncongenial sanctity.

These gentlemen sent out by the Keswick Convention have finished their mission, and, in justice to both, I have pleasure in saying that it is evident their meetings have been much appreciated. This very morning I held a long conversation with a lady of mahogany complexion, who spoke rapturously of their preaching in this place. She walked by my side quite half a mile during my matutinal walk before breakfast. Miss Sarah Walker—that was her name—informed me besides that she was unmarried, and lived with an aunt not very distant from Mandeville. I asked what her age might be.

"Thirty-one, mem," she replied.

"How do you get your living?" I asked, smiling at the pride she evidently felt at being engaged in conversation with a white lady, evidenced by the consciousness of superiority she assumed over her black sisters, who were not so honoured, and who passed on either side of us, listening politely to our conversation.

"I sit in de market, mem, and sell cakes."

"I think you all seem very well off round here," I ventured.

"Oh no, mem; there are some very poor people round 'bout," she assured me.

"But they all have coffee or oranges to sell?" I queried.

"Yes, mem; but all de summer dey get so little for der coffee, only trepence or twopence a pound, and only one and trepence for a large barrel of oranges, bery little indeed." I had already learnt that agents from the United Fruit Company buy up all the produce of the smaller cultivators in this district.

"They are so poor, mem, dey can't pay de taxes," she proceeded to inform me.

"What happens then?" I enquired.

"Den dey goes to prison, mem, or sometimes get time given dem to make up what dey can't pay."

"I suppose you have to pay rent too," I suggested.

"No, mem; we live in our own house and only pay taxes, twelve shillings and twopence ebbery year, six and a penny ebbery six munts; we go up and pay it at de Court House."

I elicited from her that she and her family had always lived in Jamaica, that once or twice she had been to Kingston, but what amused me most was her conversation upon dress.

"Bery good stuff, mem," said she, pointing to the gown which scarcely covered her knees. "I gave one and trepence a yard, and it cost four shillins for making. Last year it was Sunday frock, but when it wast it swinked up."

"I see! You like a smart frock for Sundays?" I volunteered,

having learnt that the first day of the week is special frock competition day amongst the negresses. This woman was very superior to some I met in my morning walks, who generally said, "Good morning, missus." Probably she had at one time been a domestic servant and had learnt to say "mem" for "ma'am."

"Oh yes, mem, dat's our pride; we all dress 'spectable on Sunday to go to church. Work ebbery day, but *live for Sunday*." She looked radiant at the mere thought of it.

On my return I was told that the desire to cut a fine figure every Sabbath day is the key to the labour question in Jamaica.

The negroes can live on yams, which grow in their gardens and require no trouble to cultivate, but they must work to buy the dresses good enough to wear on Sunday. On week-days they go barefoot. On Sunday they screw themselves into tight-fitting garments and into new, squeaking boots, which, if the way be long, they take off, and put on just before going into church or chapel. To be dressed smartly and go to church once a week is the highest aim of the black's life.

The fact that any white woman can ride or walk in any part of the island, either by day or by night, in perfect safety, is in itself testimony of the highest worth to the civilising agencies at work, let them be Moravian, Wesleyan, Roman or Anglican. The black under British rule is not an unworthy subject of the Empire; but left to himself, and to the workings of his own sweet will, he might perhaps revert to a state of savagery. One has only to consider the condition of the island of Hayti to see the probability of such a contingency.

I had read Chevalier St John's book on "The Black Republic," in which he mentions the cannibalistic habits of these islanders, before I left home. On two separate occasions I have since been told that the killing and eating of small children is quite a common thing, although still denied by better-class Haytians. Each of my informers were officers of ships bound for Haytian ports. There they had seen human flesh exposed for sale in the public markets. The buyers of this horrible commodity significantly ask for "salt pork." One man told me he had been taken by a Haytian of the better class to a spot at night, within forty yards of a grove, where children were being sacrificed according to the Voodhoo rites, which their ancestors practised centuries ago in the forest fastnesses of Western Africa. It was at the risk of his life. He had been unable to see the horrid rites which take place before the child was actually tomahawked, but he heard its shrieks when tortured. Great mystery surrounds the Voodhoo worship, and never, so far, has an European been known to be present at the ceremonies which take place before a human sacrifice. My informer told me that instead of dreading this fate for their children, the mothers were proud that their particular offspring should be chosen for the sacrifice.

In connection with the Haytian Voodhoo worship, I was lent an old French manuscript by an American. It had been written about one hundred and fifty years ago, and professed to be the confessions under compulsion of a Haytian negress as to the practice of the most degrading and loathsome black magic which then prevailed in the island. Whether this continues at present I am unable to say, but they still have the custom of smearing the blood of freshly-killed infants over the bodies of childless women to make them bear children. Every savage race, doubtless, at one particular stage of its development dabbled in mystic and bloody rites, just as every land, where prehistoric traces of man's existence have been found, has had its Stone Age, its kitchen-middens, etc. There is a wonderful similarity in the doings in their infancy of the world's different races, just in the same way as all children, black, brown, and white, learn to walk before they run; but to my mind it is an interesting study to see what two hundred years more or less of that which we call civilisation has produced upon a race very low down upon the evolutionary ladder. Possibly the Tierra del Fuegans and the Mincopies of the Andamans are upon the lowest rung, but I do not think an anthropologist would put the negroid races much higher up.

CHAPTER IV

THE BLACK UNDER BRITISH RULE—THE GOVERNOR OF JAMAICA AND SUITE

Without unduly congratulating ourselves as first-class colonists, I think we can fairly say that the black is at his best under British rule. He has learnt industrial arts. The best of his race are mechanics, policemen, soldiers, sailors, shopkeepers, and domestic servants. They may not be brilliant, but in this hot climate, where it is an impossibility for the European to do field labour, they serve their purpose. In Jamaica the trains and the electric trams in and round Kingston are driven by natives, your clothes are washed by negresses, and very well done too; occasionally you suffer from their excessive professional zeal, when they send home your stockings stiff with starch. The waiters, chambermaids, domestic servants, farm labourers, are all black. In the hotels it is noticeable how well they speak English.

The harmless, courteous country folk one meets in one's drives over the island are, from all accounts, very different to their dusky brethren in the United States of America, where life is none too safe, and lynch law apparently a necessary evil.

GROUP OF NATIVES.

So far as I can see, their worst fault is laziness. It is a most irritating fault to the man who wants labour; but if the pay of three days' work suffices to keep a negro in what he considers comfort, it is hard to see that he should be compelled to work six days out of seven to suit his employer's crops. And if his or her highest ambition is to cut a fine figure on Sunday, I should be inclined, whilst inculcating thrift, to encourage that amiable weakness to the uttermost. One reads sometimes of the *poor* negro, but in a country like Jamaica, where anything once planted in the soil grows in the most prolific manner, and where such nourishing food as yams and sweet potatoes form the chief nutriment of the black, to say nothing of the beautiful climate necessitating only the very lightest of clothing, real poverty, such as we are unfortunately acquainted with in England, does not exist.

Probably in a few years' time, the problem of an enormous black population will confront the government of these islands.

We know that in the United States such is the case. Barbadoes, too, has an immense population. If one thinks seriously of it, what else can be expected of a people severed from their natural state, and placed in the happiest of circumstances, where the increase of population has no such checks operating upon it, as it must have had in the wild and pristine condition of savage life amongst African forests, where a thousand petty warfares thinned the ranks of the warriors, and where cannibalism and disease would probably account for quite half the yearly tribal babies. Now, Jamaica's best crop is picaninnies. Nor are there epidemics severe enough, or earthquakes bad enough, to carry off the superfluous nigger babies.

A story which had its comical side was told me by a captain of the R.M.S. He knew a negro in Kingston who had long courted the lady of his affections. She had responded, but not to the degree demanded of her by her impassioned lover. In the captain's presence he begged her on his knees to marry him, and "make an honest man" of him.

Strangers to the West Indies are often surprised at the use of slang and funny expressions by the natives. On landing at Trinidad, we wished to be driven up to the Queen's Park Hotel for lunch. There were three of us, a lady and gentleman and myself. To our enquiry as to how much our driver would charge for taking us there, the ready answer came, "a bob each." We preserved serious faces, the driver evidently being unconscious of having said anything out of the ordinary, and paid our shillings.

I was driving one day in Kingston, when my coachman turned a sharp corner at a furious rate. In so doing, a woman was nearly run over. "Out of de way, my lub, for God's sake!" exclaimed he, not attempting to slacken his horse's pace.

There were other passengers whose eccentricities afforded the passengers of the *Port Antonio* some amusement and much subject-matter for conversation. We had the Governor of Jamaica and, according to the London newspapers, "suite" on board. In what the "suite" consisted, I am still at a loss to divine. They were the last to come on board at Avonmouth Dock, and as the rest of us who had come by an earlier train watched the small steamer, which brought them alongside the *Port Antonio*, plunging and rolling in the heavy seas which even then were racing up the Bristol Channel, we congratulated ourselves that we had walked straight on to the vessel from the quay an hour before. When their Excellencies "and suite" came on board, the ship was standing out some distance from the shore. I counted five adults, three babies, and three women-servants. The party consisted of Sir Augustus and Lady Hemming, their secretary, a married daughter with her husband, a coffee planter in Jamaica, three small children belonging to the latter, two nurses and a maid.

The present Governor of Jamaica was formerly a clerk in the office of the Secretary of State for the Colonies. In 1884 he was sent as a delegate to the West African Conference at Berlin, and later, on special service to Paris in 1890, in connection with the delimitation of French and English possessions on the west coast of Africa. He became the Governor of British Guiana, 1896, and succeeded Sir Henry Norman as Governor of Jamaica in 1898. The term of office is for five years, and this is consequently his last year in Jamaica, unless a special application is made for an extension; but one can scarcely imagine that that will be the case with Sir Augustus and Lady Hemming. Not but what it is conceded on all hands that His Excellency is a most amiable man; if not brilliant, at least he has shown conspicuous talent in the fiscal department. Owing to his clever financial administration, the island budget for the first time this year shows a surplus, although the best that can be said of the condition of Jamaica is that which Mr Chamberlain declared in the House of Commons, to the effect that up to the present the local government had been able to do little more than bring about an equipoise between revenue and expenditure.

The social relations between the chief people in the island and the reigning lady at the gubernatorial residence did not strike me as being particularly happy or satisfactory. One felt sorry that striving colonists such as the Jamaicans should lack that sympathy and consideration which, whether they be white or coloured, they certainly have a right to expect from the wives of those officials who govern them in the King's name, and who are paid very handsomely out of the island revenues for doing so.

An elderly lady who was present at a ball given last month at King's House, which is situated in lovely grounds about three miles out of Kingston, remarked to me that it was unlike entertainments of the kind given in times past, in that it lacked "grace, dignity, and refinement." I was sorry to miss this ball, but, being absent amongst the Windward Islands at the time it took place, I returned to find my invitation awaiting me at my hotel.

B. Pullen-Burry

CHAPTER V

LAND SWALLOWS—TURKS ISLANDS—AN EARTHQUAKE SHOCK—CONSTANT SPRING HOTEL

We had delightful weather some days before our arrival at Kingston; the sunsets were magnificent, the beautiful colouring of the after-glow I shall never forget. I remember two nights before the end of our journey going to the forecastle of the ship to watch the fantastic shapes of the clouds on the southern horizon, intersected as the dark masses were with the most wonderful opalesque lines of pale green, blue, and yellow, the latter shading into deepest orange. In front of us was flying a little land swallow, heralding the approach of land. As Christopher Columbus neared the scene of his wonderful discoveries, he speaks of the little winged messenger of hope which, flying on ahead of his ship, warned his brave sailors of the approach of *terra firma*.

It was no less a world-explorer than the above who discovered Jamaica the 3rd of May, 1494. It was during his second voyage to the New World, and the Spaniards kept it till 1655, when it was surrendered to an English force. Oliver Cromwell, whose policy was that of to have and to hold, sent out a Commissioner to conduct the Civil Government, also 1000 troops. These were followed shortly after by 1500 settlers from Nevis, Bermuda, New

England, and Barbadoes, and 1000 Irishmen, with as many young women. Ten years later the foundation of Jamaica's wealth as a sugar-growing country was laid by the immigration into it of over 1000 inhabitants of Surinam, which had been given to the Dutch in exchange for New York, then known as New Amsterdam; these people industriously engaged in planting sugar in the western parts of the island where the country is flat. For many years nothing more momentous than occasional depredations of a piratical nature, or attacks from French cruisers, occurred to disturb the progress of this industry.

Later the history of the island consists of constant quarrelling, the Civil Government being repeatedly repealed, then restored. Finally, in 1884, a new constitution was given to Jamaica. The present Government consists of the Governor, who is President of the Legislative Assembly, the Senior Military Officer, the Colonial Secretary, the Attorney-General, and the Director of Public Works. In addition to these are five members appointed by the Crown, and nine elected by tax-payers of upwards of twenty shillings. There are fourteen electoral districts. Jamaica—which retains the old Indian name *Xaymaca*, "a land abounding in springs"—is divided into three political divisions called counties. They are known as Middlesex, Surrey, and Cornwall respectively. These are sub-divided into fourteen parishes, the affairs of each being managed by a Parochial Board.

The Jamaican legislation has the power to pass laws applying to the Turks and Caicos Islands; the Supreme Court of Jurisdiction extending to these islands in matrimonial and divorce cases.

It was at Turks Islands that we first saw land on approaching the West Indies. They are a group lying to the south-east of the Bahamas, and were so called from a peculiar kind of cactus which grows there, somewhat resembling a Turkish fez. The largest of them is 7 miles long, and 1½ miles broad. Salt is exported from them, about 1,500,000 bushels bring annually shipped to the United States. It was midnight when we stopped and made our presence known to the Postal and Telegraph Office on shore by signalling. I looked out of my port-hole and saw a long stretch of coast, slightly hilly, but it was too indistinct to see much. The distance we were from the shore I presumed to be not more than a mile. Presently I saw a small sailing boat come close to the big steamer, and in the dim light receive an emaciated-looking mail-bag, which we had surveyed previously, when brought up to be in readiness to hand over to the postal authorities. A precocious small boy, who was permitted to feel the sealed-up bag, declared there was only one letter inside.

A stay of twenty minutes sufficed to exchange mails and to receive the latest British telegrams. Everybody was then keen to know how the Education Bill was progressing at home.

The whole of the succeeding day we coasted along the northern shores of Hayti. Universal wonder was expressed that so exquisite a spot was permitted by Providence to become that which Ruskin said of Naples, "a paradise inhabited by devils." As a nation we are suffering for the sins committed by our forefathers in bringing the "devils" away from their primeval forests. Yesterday an American lady said to me anent the negro, "He ought never to have been brought to these islands," and went on to declare that we should not only pray to be delivered from evil, but quite as much from the consequences of other people's evil, which generally fall upon the innocent more than the guilty, so I think we may profitably take thought for the morrow when we contemplate any particular course of action.

Many philanthropically-disposed persons consider that the blacks were better off under kind and considerate masters, before the days of emancipation, than in these days when each nigger does exactly as he pleases. The present situation, to my mind, seems precisely the same as that of a number of unruly schoolboys suddenly let loose from proper control and discipline.

It was the morning of Saturday, 22nd November, when we came in sight of Jamaica—but before the early hour at which everyone appeared dressed, so as not to lose the first sight of the beautiful mountainous outline—an event of some importance occurred. Bells were ringing long before daylight, and a great commotion was going on below amongst the main-deck cabins; I put on my dressing-gown, and, finding a stewardess with her arms full of soaked bedclothes, asked what on earth was the matter. Three of the cabins on the port side had been completely swamped, she told me. Since everybody had packed to be in readiness to land, it was more than awkward to have the clothes they were going to put on that morning simply saturated. One lady, whose berth lay immediately under the open port, said she had been rudely awakened by a volume of water streaming over her. Before she had recovered her breath another equally huge sea poured into the cabin; she had never been more alarmed in her life. The sea was so perfectly smooth, I could not understand it. The time was between the hours of three and four, and, so far as we knew, we were off Port Morant. However, an hour or so after, our wonder was set at rest, for the pilot who came on board to take us up Kingston Harbour advertised the fact that an earthquake shock had been felt that morning at Port Royal, and that there had not been so severe a one for thirty years. This, thought I, was a nice introduction to the volcanic sphere of action.

There is a narrow strip of land about 7 miles in length enclosing the harbour of Kingston to the southward, and Port Royal is situated at the western extremity of it. The town was, before the great earthquake of 1692, says Leslie in his Jamaican "History," the finest town in the West Indies, and at that time the richest spot in the universe. It figured in the early colonial history of this island as the emporium of the ill-gotten riches of those raiders of the Spanish Main, the buccaneers, who squandered their gains in riotous living and gambling. The wealth poured into Port Royal by these pirates was enormous. They intercepted all vessels traversing those seas. Every Spanish ship was a rich prize. If outward bound to the Indies they were laden with the choicest products and manufactures of the home country, the glass of St Ildefonso, silks and serges from Valencia, porcelain of Alcora, cordage from Carthagena, Castille soap, Toledo cutlery, the fine wool of Spain's merino sheep, with the wine and oil and almonds and raisins produced by Spain in common with Italy and the Greek islands. If they were returning home to Europe the Spanish galleons were loaded with ingots of gold and silver. The disposal of these prizes, which were numerous, made a golden harvest for the merchant; while the riot and revelry of the sailors, recklessly spending their share of the plunder, enriched the retailers; and the traffic of this far-famed mart laid the foundation of dowries for duchesses and endowments for earldoms. The Rector of Port Royal, at the time of the great earthquake, thus describes the awful occurrence: "Whole streets with their inhabitants were swallowed up by the opening of the earth, which, when shut upon them, squeezed the people to death, and in that manner several were left with their heads above ground, and others covered with dust and earth by the people who remained in the place. It was a sad sight to see the harbour covered with dead bodies of people of all conditions floating up and down without burial, for the burying-place was destroyed by the earthquake, which dashed to pieces tombs, and the sea washed the carcases of those who had been buried out of their graves." The ruins of the old city are still to be seen in clear weather under the surface of the water, and divers occasionally find relics in their explorations. Attempts to rebuild the place were frustrated first by a great fire in 1703, and subsequently by a great storm in 1722, which swept many of the buildings into the sea, destroying much shipping and many lives. On that day fifty vessels were in the harbour: out of that number four men-of-war and two merchantmen alone succeeded in getting away.

At the present day Port Royal holds an important position as a naval station. It contains the official residence of the Commodore and Staff of H.M. ships serving on the North American and West Indian station; the dockyard is fully equipped with machinery and steam-engines to repair the warships and refit them after injuries sustained. There is also a fine naval hospital, which can be made to accommodate two hundred patients if required. The defences of Port Royal have latterly been much improved, new batteries having been added to the fortifications.

It was after the fire of 1703 that Kingston, the present capital of Jamaica, began to grow in importance, a law being passed declaring that henceforth Kingston was to be the chief seat of trade and head port of entry; but the place was unpopular, and Spanish Town, built originally by the Spaniards and the seat of government, remained practically the chief town in the island for many years.

There could be nothing more beautiful than the entry into Kingston Harbour as I saw it. The Blue Mountains in the background were free from the cloudy embrace which so often veils the peaks, a lower range of hills clad with verdant green up to their summits lay between us and them. On our right was the promontory of Port Royal, with its red tiled roofs, waving palms, green foliage and yellow sands. In front, like a watch-dog, lay stretched upon the shining waters the *Urgent*, the guardship of the naval station. To our left the coast presented a semi-circular sweep, and over the green of the mangrove swamps, on which trees oysters grow, one saw in the distance the churches and warehouses of Kingston. Shortly after passing the entrance of the harbour, which is but a mile in width, a gun was fired to announce the arrival of the Direct Mail from England. Everyone was attentively admiring the beautifully situated harbour as we slowly steamed up to the company's wharf. J. T. Froude says: "The associations of the place no doubt added to the impression. Before the first hut was run up in Kingston, Port Royal was the rendezvous of all English ships which for spoil or commerce frequented the West Indian seas. Here the buccaneers sold their plunder and squandered their gains. Here in the later century of legitimate wars whole fleets were gathered to take in stores, or refit when shattered by engagements. Here Nelson had been, and Collingwood and Jervis, and all our naval heroes. Here prizes were brought in for adjudication, and pirates to be tried and hanged. In this spot more than in any other beyond Great Britain herself, the energy of the Empire was once throbbing."

Such was the past, and if the everlasting hills had looked down upon scenes of glorious days in the annals of our monarchy, as well as upon the inglorious ones of privateering, of cruelty, of rapine and of avarice, who could tell what were the possibilities of the future? Whilst we had journeyed out from England the three years of Columbian internecine warfare had drawn to a conclusion. Now there is a chance—indeed certainty, since the Americans have taken it in hand—that the Panama Canal may become a reality in years to come, instead of the failure "of the greatest undertaking of our age." When the Atlantic is united with the Pacific who can tell what future greatness lies before Kingston, being, as she is, the best harbour in the West Indies, and from her geographical situation the natural intermediate port for coaling. When this great watery highway is established, what new markets will be opened to West Indian industries!

Millions' worth of rusty machinery, never yet unpacked, lies buried in the mud of Darien, sent out when money was more plentiful than brains, and when swindling ranked with the fine arts. Thousands of lives have been lost in the swamps and jungles of the tropics over the so-far futile project of M. de Lesseps. No worse spot in the world could be found where nature resists the invasion of science and the enterprise of the European. In the hot tropical jungle, deadly snakes, alligators, mosquitoes and centipedes abound.

The unfortunate blacks, who rushed to Darien as to an expectant gold-field, attracted thither by the dollars their fellows were earning, were stricken down with yellow fever, dysentery, and typhus in countless numbers.

For all this, it has rightly been believed by many that some day, sooner or later, the commercial progress of the world will demand the execution of this apparently impossible scheme. Now we confidently look to America to see it successfully completed.

To return to the world of actualities, I gazed interestedly down from the decks of the *Port Antonio* to the quay where we were to land. The mahogany-coloured occupants of numerous small boats shouted up to us, gesticulating and laughing as they showed their beautiful white teeth. Meanwhile, the great ship slowly approached her moorings. Then a detachment of a West

Indian regiment, marching to the sound of a band, approached, and took up a position exactly in front of us.

Directly the gangway was accessible a troop of officials thronged up on deck to pay their respects to the Governor. The band struck up a popular air, the soldiers were inspected, and Sir Augustus Hemming with his friends passed out of sight. People came streaming on board to greet their home-returning relatives and friends, whilst every religious community seemed to be represented in the motley groups of black-coated men who had come to receive the delegates from Keswick.

"They are going to have a high old time," irreverently remarked a stray black sheep amongst my fellow-passengers, speaking collectively of the black-garbed ecclesiastics. I found some friends waiting for me, who very kindly steered me and my belongings through the custom-house, which is quite close to the landing-stage, and proved to be no ordeal whatever, since I had no merchandise to account for. My trunks were given into the care of a porter from Constant Spring Hotel, and I had no farther trouble with them. My friends got a "bus," as the buggies are called in Kingston, and we drove a very short distance, when I entered the electric tram which every twenty minutes runs between the town and the hotel, six miles away.

For the benefit of intending visitors to Jamaica I may here mention that Messrs Elder, Dempster & Co., who own the Direct Mail Service by which I travelled, and which some two years ago was called into existence by Mr Chamberlain in his efforts to help the West Indies, are also the proprietors of the two best hotels Jamaica possesses: Myrtle Bank in the town of Kingston, and Constant Spring, 6 miles off in the country.

My intention was to go first of all to the latter, especially as

I heard how hot Kingston is in the daytime. I learnt, too, that a voucher from Constant Spring Hotel enabled you to take what meal you chose at their other hotel in town and *vice versa*. I had several purchases to make, so that if I were to be busy shopping in the heat of the day, so much the more advantageous would it be to ensure cool nights.

I cannot say that I admire Kingston; in fact I consider all West Indian towns best at a distance. The electric trams are a great boon, and an eminently satisfactory mode of transit. The American lady of smoking-room fame joined me *en route* for the hotel. She could not refrain, when she saw the sugar-cane as we passed the market, from buying some. She said it reminded her of her home in California, and, much to the amusement of the blacks opposite, she brought out a knife and insisted on teaching me how to eat cane. This was my first acquaintance with Jamaican blacks; but I still turn round to admire the country women striding along with Heaven only knows what in those heaped-up baskets on their heads, to which they seem to give not a thought. For the most part, they wear clean print gowns, short, fastened up below the waist behind, so as not to impede their gait—I have since read that no women in the world walk better or can poise such weights on their heads as they can. Very charming country houses with nice gardens line the road, when once one is out of the town right away to Constant Spring. We paid fourpence for our ride, and at the end of it, walked up a path sheltered with trellised arches, and covered with alamander, bougainvillia, scarlet hibiscus, with nicely laid-out gardens on each side of us, arriving in due course at the central entrance of the hotel. Having secured rooms adjoining, with verandahs looking out on to the garden, and beyond that the golf links, which we learnt, together with a new wing, were to be opened in a few days, we repaired to the spacious dining-room, which takes the whole breadth of the building, as indeed do all the sitting-rooms. Thus, with balconies on either side, one can always find a cool spot. My friend and I chose a table and ordered lunch. The fair Delicia swept ponderously past us.

"Oh! won't you come and lunch with us?" asked my companion in the kindest manner.

"Thank you," returned that important spinster in acrid accents; "I have my own table prepared for me," and she followed the manager to another part of the room, where henceforth she was always to be seen alone in her grandeur.

"My goodness!" exclaimed the charming American, when her pomposity had betaken herself to a safe distance, "if I'd guessed she was that crabby I'd have saved my breath. She has put on empty-headed side since she struck this hotel!"

Several of our fellow-passengers found their way up to Constant Spring during the course of the afternoon. The little journalist made tracks for the fair Delicia.

We found some nice people staying at the hotel, amongst them the inevitable British matron, who was shocked at so many things that I wondered how it was she could stay in a land where so much human anatomy is in evidence, as it certainly is in this island.

For people who want a warm climate to winter in, pleasant society, and a comfortable hotel in which to stay, I consider Constant Spring Hotel a very charming resort. The building is large, and extends over a good deal of ground. You enter a large central hall, where small tables used for afternoon tea are scattered about, with most comfortable chairs and lounges. The staircases on either side lead to a gallery above, from which you look down upon the scene below. From this hall, on your right, you pass through the large drawing-room to the dining-room; on your left, you enter into the reading-room, which is nicely fitted up with half-a-dozen writing tables, whilst a table in the centre is covered with magazines and papers; this room is carpeted throughout, so that persons walking through do not disturb you when reading or writing. Passing through this room you come to the ping-pong and billiard-rooms. Another great advantage is that there is a first-rate swimming bath belonging to the hotel, and which is open to both ladies and gentlemen at certain hours. The expenses of a winter residence in this hotel would not be greater than at any similar one in the south of France, about fifteen shillings a day; but for a permanent stay, or visit of some weeks, advantageous terms could be made. I should advise people writing from England and engaging rooms to be careful to ask for them on the north side, which is the cool side, looking out towards the Blue Mountains. Visitors to Jamaica, coming out with introductions to a few residents, would soon find themselves in very pleasant society at Kingston, and during the winter months there are a good many garden-parties, dinners, and dances, both at the hotels and in the neighbourhood.

Besides the naval station at Port Royal there is a garrison at Newcastle which is situated some 4000 feet above sea-level; it appears that formerly our soldiers were quartered in mangrove swamps: the Government has of late years gone to the opposite extremes. Now their habitation is amongst the clouds. There is no doubt about the healthy situation of this eyrie in the mountains; but one pities the poor fellows condemned to an exile of two or three years in this isolated spot. The temperature in this elevated region never rises beyond 70° and never drops below 60°. The officers, although they can descend occasionally from the misty heights, must be bored beyond description. There is absolutely nothing to hunt, nothing to shoot; the mongoose has eaten up every partridge, as it has exterminated snakes, and driven the remaining rats into dwelling-houses.

B. Pullen-Burry

CHAPTER VI

SUITABLE CLOTHING—PEDESTRIANS IN JAMAICA—SELF-HELP SOCIETY

Before I launch out into ecstasies over the tropical scenery, and the luxuriant multiplicity of the flora of this island, I intend to rid my memory of certain precautionary information with which I consider, at this juncture, it will be well to acquaint any reader who may be meditating a visit to this part of the world.

In the matter of dress I advise those who wish to see the island scenery to leave their heavy luggage at either of the hotels they choose to stay at when first landing. Since the interior parts of the island are in many places only accessible either on horseback, as to houses high up in the Blue Mountains, or as Mandeville, by long drives in buggies from the railway stations, it is advisable to carry only a limited amount of what one absolutely requires in bags, portmanteaus, or bundles tightly strapped in waterproof cases. I cannot do better than warn persons of the tropical rains which are so frequent in the West Indian islands. Do not time your visit either in May or October, for these are the rainy months, but you are always liable to sudden outpourings at other times of the year and in the finest weather. These rains drench you to the skin often before you can find shelter, and the danger of catching fever is great if you do not at once change your wet clothing. Personally, I consider the waterproof cloak which Messrs Elvery In Conduit

Street, W., supply for tropical countries about the most suitable that I have seen. For everyday wear, washing skirts and blouses, the latter without lining, are by far the best; a light, fine serge dress will be useful for a sojourn amongst the mountains where fires are sometimes necessary in the evening, and blankets are slept under. The true test of the Jamaican climate is whether or not one can sleep under a woollen cover. Shady hats, and one or two silk dresses for evening or Sunday wear, are about as much as one wants for a tourist's visit of six weeks to a couple of months.

If, however, you come out to spend the winter at Constant Spring Hotel and expect to go much into society, you cannot bring out too many smart gowns, or too much flummery in the shape of millinery, for the heat soon takes the freshness off your airiest confections. Let the gowns, however, be such as you would wear in the hottest summer in England, and you will then be fairly near the mark.

Whilst I am speaking on the subject of dress I may as well acquaint you with the fact that muslins and cottons are to be bought here as reasonably as they are in England. Some people say they are cheaper, and are made and exported especially for colonial use. This probably is a correct version, when it is taken into consideration that by law all the blacks have to provide themselves with decent clothing. With the women, this always takes the form of cotton, either as print, drill, piqué, or muslin. There are very fair dressmakers, who are certainly very moderate in their charges, to be found at Kingston. They are excellent copyists and clever machinists. Provided they have a good pattern they will turn out a well-made skirt for about six shillings, and a blouse for a little less. Many people coming out from England employ them, and there is this to be said in their favour, they do not keep you waiting long for your dresses, but generally send them to you in two or three days.

Another important item to be considered in a visit to Jamaica is boots. Some persons tell you to get a size larger, both in gloves and shoes, than your ordinary sizes for coming out here. At any rate, provide yourself with soft kid boots coming high up the leg, to protect your ankles from the insects which seem by preference to attack that particular part of your limbs. At Kingston the mosquitoes are virulent, here at Mandeville there are scarcely any. But far worse than these are the ticks which render it positively dangerous to walk in long grass, or to gather at random from the country hedges as you take your walks. These obnoxious insects are the curse of the island; they attack both man and beast. Years ago West Indians say they roamed as children about the hills and woods, gathering what wild flowers they liked, never thinking or troubling about these insects. Now the nurses have strict injunctions not to let the children wander in long grass for fear of the noisome little pests. The introduction of foreign cattle into Jamaica some twenty-five years ago accounts for their presence; since then they have increased and multiplied till they are a positive plague. In the *Port Antonio* we brought out a number of starlings sent by Sir Alfred Jones, who is the moving spirit of Elder, Dempster & Co., and who is most energetic in his attempts to benefit the island. This gentleman hopes they may acquire a taste for ticks in the same way the mongoose on its arrival in Jamaica devoted his attentions to the extermination of rats and snakes. It would indeed be a good thing if they could be got rid of. I hear that another gentleman having the same object in view has imported a lot of common hedge-sparrows. The poor starlings we brought out with us suffered terribly from sea-sickness, scarcely half of them surviving the journey. The timorous-hearted may be thankful that there is nothing in the animal or reptile world to be afraid of in country rambles. At home we have poisonous snakes, here there are none. There are lizards, but the natives eat them, and also the land crab. Scorpions are rarely met with, and are not considered so dangerous here as elsewhere. Ants and sand-flies are found in the low-lying lands. The most charming live things are the beautiful little humming-birds often seen trembling over sweet-smelling tree blossoms. I have often watched them flitting over flowering acacia bushes. There are twenty different sorts of these enumerated by a naturalist called Goese. Those I have generally seen have bright bodies of metallic shimmering peacock green, with black feathers on the head, tail and back.

To return to the subject of dress. Gentlemen will find their summer suits and flannels indispensable; they should also provide themselves with good macintoshes.

For an athlete, or indeed for anybody possessed of good walking powers, it is not impossible to take a walking trip over part of this island—especially as there are small weekly boats starting from Kingston every Tuesday, stopping at the various ports and harbours as they make the circuit of Jamaica. These call at each place for fruit on behalf of the American Fruit Company, whose boats run between Port Antonio and Boston, New York, Philadelphia, and Baltimore. The chief harbours are Port Morant, Kingston, Old Harbour, Green Island, Montego Bay, Falmouth, Port Maria, St Ann's Bay, Lucea, and Port Antonio; these boats stop at all these. The island of Jamaica itself is only 144 miles at its extreme length, and its greatest width is 49 miles. From Kingston to Annotto Bay on the north coast it is only 21½ miles. The roads are exceptionally good throughout, thanks to Sir H. A. Blake, and there is no reason why a good pedestrian should not fix upon Jamaica as a fitting spot to be done on shankses' pony, provided always he be suitably dressed, and commences his peregrinations at sunrise, rests from 11 A.M. to 4 P.M., and takes up his journey then till dusk, or as far into the night as he pleases. The same applies to bicycling and to riding on horseback.

FRUIT STEAMER ON ITS WEEKLY ROUND.

There is this to be said to people who cannot accommodate themselves to somewhat primitive conditions of existence, or who are not in the enjoyment of at least moderately good health: they should not come to the West Indies at all. In the first place, the excessive heat in the middle of the day is decidedly trying; even the strongest take some time to become acclimatised. Then the food is not the same as English people are used to—that is, in the country lodging-houses and hotels. To this day I abstain from salt-fish and akee, a favourite West Indian breakfast dish; nor can I acquire a taste for the Avocado pear, which is eaten as a salad, but which to me seems identical with soft soap. Papaw too, which is handed round for dessert, I find as unpalatable as mangoes;

both the latter are, however, considered delicious by West Indians notwithstanding the flavour of turpentine which characterises the latter. Yams are nice; they resemble potatoes. The garden egg and Cho Choes are also acceptable, the latter resembling greatly our vegetable marrow.

At Constant Spring Hotel I first became acquainted with Jamaican fruits, and the profusion and quantity of them, together with their cheapness, constitute one of the most agreeable features in the island housekeeping. Grape fruit, delicious tangerines, too ripe for export, juicy pines, cool water-melons, bananas *ad lib.*, were always piled up in a big central dish on our breakfast table. Along the road-sides here, at Mandeville, from whence I am writing these pages, oranges and grape fruit fall off the trees, and nobody considers it worth their while to pick them up. The waste of ripe fruit seems enormous, where the means of transit are not present to convey it to a shipping port.

One of the most delicious things they give you at this hotel is guava jelly served with cocoa-nut cream. Indeed the table is unexceptionally good, also both at Myrtle Bank and Constant Spring.

The day following my arrival being Sunday I did not leave the hotel, but completed a somewhat large correspondence I wanted to send *viâ* America. Letters sent to England *viâ* the Atlas Steamship Company's vessels to the States reach home in twelve days; you can also send them by the Direct Mail and the Royal Mail Service. There are innumerable places of worship, not only in Kingston but all over the island; in fact the Church of England, Roman Catholics, Presbyterians, Wesleyans, Methodists, and Moravians, all do their best to keep the population in that narrow path where to convince them of sin seems to be the favourite doctrine. No doubt the attractions of the broad way which leads to destruction require pointing out vigorously to the semi-heathen intelligence; but from expositions I heard in nonconformist chapels, I wondered what form of amusement was left open to "believers."

Once I was present at Cambridge when a venerable American bishop, since dead, but known as the "Apostle of the Indians," uttered the following words, which I have never forgotten. The occasion was the centenary of a religious society. Preachers of different persuasions had spoken of the advance of the society in their own particular sectarian sphere. "Far be it from me to present to the heathen a divided Christianity!" I hear that the puzzled wits of the woolly-haired race do give way occasionally under the strain of theological pressure. I travelled with a poor black, afflicted with religious mania, from St Thomas to Antigua, and a doctor told me that there was a good deal of it amongst the natives.

As I had several purchases to make and to expedite by the *Port Antonio* on its homeward passage, I prepared myself for a long day's shopping on Monday, and indeed I did very little else before going to the first official garden-party at King's House on the Friday following my arrival.

The town of Kingston has been called in my hearing "a collection of shanties," and although I will not give my assent quite to this appellation, I cannot honestly admire it. Fine buildings it certainly lacks. The chief street is Harbour Street, and having once found that, the other streets run either at right angles or parallel with it.

My first commission was to order a number of tortoiseshell articles, which are made here cheaply and well by a man called Andrews. Then it is a nice thing to know that you can send your friends a box containing a hundred oranges properly packed for the sum of twelve shillings, provided they do not live beyond a certain distance from London. Blue Mountain coffee is also an acceptable present. Experts declare that there is no better in the world; and whether it be true or not I cannot tell, but I learnt from apparently reliable authority that the Czar is supplied entirely with the product of one of these upland plantations. Guava jelly made in the island is delicious, and often sent home by request of those who have known it out here. Indeed I think many families with delicate-chested members might do worse than live, for a while at least, in Jamaica. House-rent in the upper part of the town is not dear, and the houses are well built, all of them being surrounded with gardens of varying size, where bougainvillia, hibiscus, palm-trees, and the crimson-leaved poin-settia are nearly always to be seen. The rents of these vary from £50 to £100, according to size. They have three postal deliveries per diem. Fruit, vegetables and fish are cheap, and prices generally most moderate; for instance, beef is sixpence a pound, pork, ninepence, bread, threepence, sugar, twopence, coffee, one shilling, fish, sixpence. The dearest articles of diet are ham, at eighteenpence, tea, three shillings, good butter, eighteenpence to two shillings, English cheese, eighteenpence. Fruit and vegetables are not worth mentioning; pines are to be had for twopence, and for a penny you can get a dozen bananas. The native produce is of course cheap, and you pay more in proportion for imported goods. A buggy to hold four persons costs, when new, about £40, and you can buy sufficiently good horses from £15 to £20, and even cheaper; but the town of Kingston and environs is so well served by the tramway service, and the hire of buggies within the urban limits so cheap, that it is quite possible to live comfortably in the suburbs without a conveyance. The streets are well lighted by gas, some of the hotels and public buildings by electricity. Labour is not a very dear item either; the working hours are from 6 A.M. to 5 P.M., with an hour off, between 11 and 12 o'clock. On Saturdays no work is done after 11 o'clock. Labourers are paid from eighteenpence to two shillings a day, women from ninepence to one shilling. Many of the domestic servants live away from the houses, coming early in the morning, and leaving about nine in the evening. In a great many households the mistress does not feed the women-servants. If there are several, they have a room to eat in, providing for themselves; and I should imagine this was by far the best way, for the nauseous compounds in their stock-pots, when they thus choose their own provender, are unsuitable to the stomach of any average English domestic servant. Salt-fish in an advanced stage of decay is a favourite dish with them, but nothing comes amiss, and all finds its way into the big pot.

There are not many curios to be bought in any of the West Indian islands, but for what few there are it is best to go to the Women's Self-Help Society. Here you can get lamp-shades, doyleys, mats of all descriptions made from lace-bark, and ferns artistically arranged; long chains for the neck, or muff, made from native seeds dried and strung together. Those which are mostly bought are known locally as "Job's Tears" and "Women's Tongues." There was a great run on these a week or two back when Dr Lunn's tourist steamer, the *Argonaut*, put into Kingston Harbour, and its passengers, to the number of a hundred and thirty, spent £70 on the island curiosities. Great joy reigned amongst the lady promoters of the Society: such a windfall does not often happen to them.

This "Women's Self-Help Society" was founded by Lady Musgrave, the wife of a former Governor, and was opened in 1879. Apparently there are a number of what some of our papers at home are pleased to designate as decayed gentlewomen in

Jamaica, and the object of this industry is to find a sale for all kinds of work which they, when industriously inclined, are able to do. There is, however, an agency attached to it whereby distressed needlewomen can get orders to execute for ladies and gentlemen, and there is a stock of clothes always kept ready, suitable for servants and working people.

The latest Handbook of Jamaica says of this institution: "The Society has been a great boon to many people in reduced circumstances who have to work for their living, but find it difficult to get suitable employment. It also enables other women, who do not require the profit of their work for themselves, to earn something for charities and philanthropic objects, as well as to raise the standard of work by bringing to bear on it that cultivated taste and artistic grace which is the natural result of a refined education." So much for this Society and its aims. I should mention that the seeds called "Women's Tongues" are those which hang in long pods from a tree called ponciana. When the seeds are dry, and the wind blows the boughs of the trees, they rattle in the pods, hence the title. "Job's Tears" are the seeds of a plant which bends by the water-edge, its melancholy attitude having given rise to the name.

CHAPTER VII

DOMINICA'S FLOURISHING CONDITION—SCOTCH DINNER—TROPICAL VEGETATION

Two or three days after my arrival at Constant Spring Hotel, I began to feel that my West Indian experiences would lack any degree of thoroughness if I did not include a journey to the Windward and Leeward Islands; how to get to them I had yet to learn.

I longed to set eyes on the volcanoes. Mont Pelée was said to be continually throwing up huge masses of incandescent lava, which, constantly rolling down her smoking sides, was altering her geographical shape, and choking up a contiguous river-bed.

The French Government had prohibited any landing at St Pierre, but a scientific expedition under Professor La Croix had the pluck to live in a temporarily constructed observatory at the base of the mountain; always, I learnt afterwards, in readiness to fly at the approach of danger. The undermining of the cone going on within the crater threatened further eruption, ashes ejected having a temperature of 100° Centigrade, after a week's cooling. Eyewitnesses gave graphic descriptions of the abomination of desolation which La Soufrière had worked upon the fertile districts of the north part of St. Vincent as we sat in the spacious central hall of Constant Spring Hotel, whilst estate-owners of Jamaica indulged in jeremiads over the financial depression reigning here. They pointed in envy to the flourishing condition of the little island of Dominica, where it is apparent that a West Indian colony can get along without sugar. It was inspiriting to read how that beautiful and well-favoured possession of the Crown was forging ahead, in spite of the Royal Mail Steamship Company's prohibitive freight charges, and the Sugar Bounties. Apparently people with moderate capital have been attracted there sufficiently to purchase Crown lands. This is exactly what Jamaica needs. The cry here for central sugar factories and new-fashioned plant instead of obsolete machinery is a loud cry, but that for capital and new blood is still louder. In Dominica men have had sufficient means to sit down quietly between the planting of their cocoa trees and its yielding remunerating returns, a matter of from five to six years.

One Jamaican paper says of this island: "Its happy condition is enough to make a Jamaican gasp with envy. The revenue in 1901 amounted nearly to £30,000, the highest ever realised in the island. There was no increase of taxation, the improvement being entirely due to the development of trade, and the increased purchasing power of the people. Although considerable sums were spent in the reconstruction and improvement of roads, and in other public works, the year closed with an accumulated surplus of nearly £6000. Of this amount £4000 have been invested as a reserve fund. Think of Jamaica with a reserve fund! How does Dominica manage it? So far as we can see, it has ceased to cultivate sugar. During the last decade it has cultivated cocoa, and produced lime-juice and its bye-products. The value of its cocoa exports has risen from £7000 to £24,000, while the shipment of lime-juice in 1901 was valued locally at £35,000. It has also gone in for rubber, vanilla, oranges, and other minor products."

People who are to be believed tell me that the percentage of juice extracted from the cane is 50 per cent. below that attainable with modern machinery in many parts of the West Indies. It is obvious that until up-to-date appliances are substituted for the crude and obsolete methods of manufacture, the sugar industry has no prosperous outlook before it, nor can it hope to compete with beet sugar.

My intention to visit these islands soon shaped itself. I found a couple of fellow-passengers were going up to St Thomas in the Danish West Indies by the Royal Mail steamships, this being their coaling and repairing station, in reality the *ultima thule* of their inter-colonial voyages in these parts.

I arranged, therefore, to leave in a week's time on the s.s. *Para*. In the meantime, I hoped to see something of the country round Kingston, leaving the rest of the island to be visited at the end of December.

The intervening days passed away very pleasantly at Constant Spring Hotel. There was a dance on the Monday evening; in fact, all through the winter season there is a weekly gathering of this description. Officers from the camp, and the principal residents to the number of about forty, were present on this occasion. Very good music was supplied by the four musicians who are engaged to play every afternoon in the hotel drawing-room, a pianist, a violincello player, and two violinists. Some pretty frocks were worn, many of the girls appearing in delicate muslin gowns, evidently locally made, but quite adequate to the occasion.

Another day a dinner was given to all the Scotchmen in Jamaica, in honour of their national saint. The ubiquitous Scot is to be found all over creation. There is a story going, that when some enterprising explorer finds his way to the North Pole, he will find a Scot warming himself at a fire there. About one hundred and fifty sat down to a veritable Scotch repast. The Governor was the guest of the evening. Visitors staying at the hotel sat in the verandah outside the dining-room, and listened with interest to the after-dinner speeches. Before they got to that stage, the national dish, the haggis, was duly honoured, being carried round in triumph, preceded by the bagpipes, played by a very stately-looking piper. This was greeted by the guests with exceeding enthusiasm. Some of the speeches were quite eloquent, notably so was that of Dr. Gordon, the Roman Catholic Bishop. He was called upon to answer to the toast to "bonnie Scotland." One felt borne away in the spirit to the land of Burns and Rob Roy, as he led his hearers mentally at a canter over hill and dale, and across swiftly flowing burns fringed with mountain ash, and then plunged them into the gloom of mountain fastnesses and forest depths. It was time, however, to come back to the West Indies at last, and, when the Bishop sat down, his word-painting of highland scenery earned for him an enthusiastic ovation. After that a guest with a considerable flow of language alluded to the fact that "Governors come" and "Governors go," but that they (the Jamaicans) "went on for ever." Sir Augustus Hemming is certainly possessed of tact, and, whenever I have heard him speak, generally seems to say the correct thing. On this occasion, once or twice things were said which were not quite in good taste, but His Excellency adroitly skidded over risky topics, ignoring that which had been said, but which it would be better in such a gathering to have left unsaid.

I have not yet mentioned the impression I received on my first drives and walks in Jamaica. The colouring is superb. To an artistic mind, there is scarcely an hour in the day, when looking on to the hills at the back of the hotel, that a beautiful view is not to be obtained. Sometimes the mountain summits are veiled in white mists, but at sunset the colours are grand, and for that only are, to my mind, worth the journey to Jamaica. The foliage and the parasitical growth, the hanging festoons which drape from tree to tree, must be seen to be appreciated. Tropical vegetation is in all its glory here. Innumerable ferns and palm-trees wave in the air along the banks of the well-kept roads. Plantains and bananas rear their ragged leaves against the sky. Exquisitely green cedars (not those we know) are a beautiful feature of the landscape, with orange-trees bearing blossom and fruit simultaneously. Tamarinds and gums spring from rocky crags, shrubs and creepers are everywhere; the latter intertwine themselves in the most wonderful way over tree parasites, back again to the road bank, then you trace them twenty yards or so further on, embracing gigantic stems. Not a single tree seems familiar. One feels as if one were always walking in a botanical garden; the wealth of flowering plants, of edible fruit and vegetables, strikes one wherever one goes. How refreshing and how nourishing are the articles of food which Nature, in an open-handed generosity, not to be found in less favoured climes, scatters broadcast over these islands! If negroes have yams, bread-fruit, oranges, bananas, cocoa-nuts, growing at their back door without the trouble of cultivating them—for anything once stuck into the ground will grow—how can you expect them to work six days out of seven?

Yesterday I was talking to a coffee-planter, who owns a large property in this neighbourhood. I asked him how he got on with his blacks, for no two planters seem to me to agree in their opinions as to the capabilities of their work-people.

"I don't have any trouble with them," he replied. "I pay 'em well because I find it suits me best, but as to ever imagining they will make decent citizens, why, it's out of the question! The fools might have bought us all out by this time, if they had any sense."

"And made the island a second Hayti?" I suggested.

"Well, possibly! but when they do buy a bit of land they ruin it by bad cultivation," said he.

"I wish they would not live crowded up together in those filthy one-roomed huts! I cannot get over my feeling of disgust at them in this respect!"

"They might take a bath sometimes!" he interrupted. "They have not any decent pride." He went on to speak of their very sketchy covering at coffee harvesting time, and said he never let his women-folk go near them on those occasions.

This gentleman had been in Jamaica since 1876. Sugar, he said, had ruined his family. Coffee was the only crop he considered worth cultivating. There was no money in oranges—this conclusion I had arrived at myself.

It was about this time I paid my first visit to Hope Gardens. I went with a friend who knew one of the officials, and we were taken all over that interesting government establishment for the promotion of agriculture. Here plants are introduced, and, if suitable to the climate and soil, are propagated. The products of Jamaica being purely agricultural, the well-organised and scientifically-treated garden and plantations are of great help to students. Early last century yams, cocoas, maize, and plantains, etc., were first cultivated, so as to make the island less dependent upon American supplies; they are spoken of as valuable exotics. Indeed it is interesting to learn where Jamaica obtained her inexhaustible products. In Bryan Edward's "History of the British West Indies," vol. 1, p. 475, we are told that in 1782 the mango, akee, cinnamon, camphor, jack-tree, kola, date-palm, rose-apple, turmeric, and other valuable plants to the number of six hundred had been not only introduced, but acclimatised in Jamaica.

Spain furnished oranges, lemons, limes, and citrons. The prickly pear came from Mexico. The shaddock from China. Guinea-grass, which is most useful for cattle, was accidentally brought from the west coast of Africa. Sugar-cane was grown here by the Spaniards, but first cultivated by the English in 1660. Logwood came from Honduras; this is a famous dye-wood and has a beautiful blossom. The graceful bamboo was brought from Hispaniola. The scarlet flowering akee, eaten as a vegetable, came from West Africa in a slaver. Pimento is indigenous to the island; from this tree we get allspice. The fustic tree, from which khaki dye is produced, is common along the hedgerows; so is also aniseed, which is known medicinally in most of our English homes. The nutmeg tree is quite common in the West Indies. In Hope Gardens they have specimens of every plant grown in the island, and for those fond of botany, I can imagine nothing more enjoyable than to wander for hours amongst its trees and plants. Connected with this government institution the Jamaican Agricultural Society make special grants for lectures.

Practical demonstrations on bee-keeping have been made throughout the island, and Jamaica honey is considered one of the best which reaches the London market.

Personally, I consider the bread-fruit tree, the Jamaican cedar, the beautiful clumps of feathery bamboos, about the most beautiful of the trees generally met with in country drives. As one walks along the grass bordering the road, one may inadvertently step upon the sensitive plant, which curls up when touched; but one's attention is incessantly aroused at the wonderful growth of cacti and orchids, and what the natives call "wild pines," lining the boughs of the trees, and fixing themselves in great clumps in the forks of the branches. The *Palma Christi*, or castor-oil plant, grows wild.

Farming here is called pen-keeping, and in some districts there are very fine grazing lands. In fact, it seems to me that no more productive ground exists under Heaven. If the people had more energy as well as more capital, it ought to be a little Paradise, barring the ticks. A relative of mine described the state of Jamaica very aptly when he said, "The indifference of the blacks was only equalled by the apathy of the Europeans."

CHAPTER VIII
SAVINGS BANKS—KESWICK VIEWS—SPANISH TOWN

I have been interrupted in my writing this morning by listening to a very entertaining conversation going on between two maid-servants, both pure negresses, as to whether pink or blue chiffon would look best in their Sunday hats. The latest fashion is to see smartly-dressed black ladies with well-powdered necks and faces, wearing huge knots of coloured ribbon on the left breast. Everything they can save goes to buy finery. Out of four shillings a week, three are spent on dress, the fourth feeds them. Much is done to induce them to put spare pence into savings banks, which were established as early as 1837, depositors receiving 4½ per cent.; but some years after, a panic ensued, when the secretary of a branch bank committed forgery, and was sentenced to fourteen years' penal servitude.

In 1870 a Government savings bank supplanted the former; the interest depositors get now is only 2½ per cent. The married negress lawfully regards her deposits as her own special property. That this is a praiseworthy as well as useful institution is proved by the fact that there were on the 31st of March 1900 32,860 depositors, including charities, societies, clubs and public functionaries investing in their official capacities. To assist people to deposit smaller sums, there are now penny banks established in different parts of the island by influential persons and clergymen. In 1897 there were forty-three of these with 11,703 depositors. The currency is the same as in England, but there are nickel pennies in circulation and paper notes for sovereigns. I studiously avoid taking the latter, and insist on English gold: the dirty things are detestable. Yesterday I went into a store at Mandeville to buy some trifle, and I saw two black damsels trying the effect of transparent muslin over their dusky arms; that with the biggest pattern was chosen, it was "preetty fe trew," they thought.

I am indebted to a Kingston clergyman for many amusing negro stories; having lived here over thirty years he has quite a fine collection. This is one. A negro stood chatting with the blacksmith in his shop. After a while he broke out, "Hi, me smell fire burn!" With a frightful exclamation he gave a jump, and found he had been standing on a piece of iron just out of the fire, but it had taken some time for the heat to penetrate the hoof!

A coloured man wrote thus to a clergyman:—

> "Dear Minister,—My mother is dead, and expects to be buried this afternoon at four o'clock. Please come and administer over her remains."

GARDEN AT MYRTLE BANK HOTEL.

Another story tells of an irreligious young clerk who often teased one of the head men about his piety and church-going. On Monday morning the chaff began as usual.

"You went to church again yesterday, you old rascal."

"Yes, buckra," replied he, "me go a church, sah! but de trange ting is me hear 'bout you, sah, during service."

"Yes, you hear about me, eh!"

"Yes, sah, parson read de word, 'De fool hat said in his heart dere is no god.'"

One day I read in the newspapers that the Keswick delegates were to give their last service at Kingston, before setting off on an evangelising tour throughout the island.

A fellow-passenger on the *Port Antonio* said he would like to hear them. We arranged to dine at Myrtle Bank Hotel, and go afterwards to the place of worship where the service was to take place. This hotel has an entrance into it from Harbour Street; the gardens on the other side of the building go down to the water's edge, and are cool and inviting. Generally a breeze, known as "the doctor," from the sea is blowing, which makes it deliciously refreshing.

We dined shortly after six, and were whirled in a "'bus" for sixpence to Coke Chapel, a large edifice furnished with galleries. Crowds were fighting to get in. Fortunately, the official black is still imbued with the idea of the superiority of the white people, but how long that will last if the social democrat is allowed to preach the equality of the black with the white, is a question a wiser head than mine may solve. On this occasion, my friend and I were shown with much respect to seats near the pulpit. There were mostly coloured people in our immediate vicinity; a little further away faces of ebony and mahogany made up the rest of the large congregation. All looked serious, expectant, prosperous, too, if one were justified in judging by the clothes they wore. The service began by a hymn, followed by extempore prayer. The singing was congregational and hearty. The blacks love singing hymns; one hears old familiar tunes hummed constantly wherever one goes.

But the addresses were what they all came for. The delegates from Keswick were both good speakers, and they fairly riveted the attention of their hearers. However, a more unpractical Christianity, a more uninviting picture of the religious life as laid down by these Evangelists, it has never been my lot to listen to. Calvin and Knox flourished over three centuries ago. Revivalists nowadays preach on gentler lines.

These childish, ignorant, irresponsible, but happy-hearted children of the South were told that smoking, drinking, card-playing, dancing-parties, love-making, novel-reading, society-going were incompatible with the Christian life. If they wanted to enjoy such things they were imperatively bidden to leave the church. In this instance, that meant membership of nonconformist bodies. I learnt from the local newspapers, which indiscriminately praised the work of the delegates, that they upheld a high standard of spiritual life. It may be so. But of what use is it to describe the unattainable and the impossible, seeing that negro human nature is limited in its perceptions and in its capabilities, and a white man would think twice before he made such wholesale renunciations! The young women present were enjoined to keep themselves to themselves; they were not to seek husbands, the Lord would provide them! What about English church-going spinsters? I wondered. Many of them had not *chosen* the better part.

That they should not desire to go into society was impressed upon them, since that often led to trouble. To exemplify this teaching the Old Testament story of Dinah as given in Genesis was taken as the text. I have since looked it up. It belongs to the unreadable stories of the Pentateuch, but the gist of it, as presented to the mixed assembly, was, that Dinah, said the preacher, probably like many in front of him, "wanted more society than home afforded, so she called to see the daughters of the land." Just in the same way they might go to tea at different houses in Kingston. Harm came of it, for she met somebody who got her into trouble, and the end of it was her lover was killed. The moral of the story was obvious. Safety was only to be found in staying at home! Practical persons say the best teaching for these people is that of example. If they see English people live well-ordered lives, they will in time learn to copy them in the same way as they copy English dress. Many of them are really stupid; they seem unable to retain what they hear. A lady tells me that her servants can never repeat the text, nor give a reasonable account of what they have heard at church. She asked a girl who had that day been to Sunday School, it being Whit Sunday:

"Who is the Comforter you heard about?"

The lady who taught the class was the clergyman's wife.

"Judas Iscariot, missus," promptly and unabashed came the reply.

And this, she tells me, is a specimen of how they jumble up Bible names and stories. No doubt there is a physiological solution to this muddle-headedness, but it must be particularly trying for those who would like to really improve them.

The next day I went with several people from the hotel to a garden-party at King's House. The afternoon was very hot; fortunately it became slightly cooler by 4.30: the reception was from half-past four to six o'clock. Their Excellencies received us at the entrance of the gardens. Guests to the number of about one hundred and fifty had arrived; very few government officials were present, and altogether, as a representative gathering of the best people in the island, I admit we did not think much of it. A lady resident told me the cause of so limited a number taking the trouble to come was of course the unpopularity of the lady who presides over the entertaining at King's House. We chatted to those we knew, strolled about the grounds. The house, which is unpretentious, is situated in a hundred acres, containing some beautiful shrubs and rare plants. Refreshments were served under the trees. It grew dark. We sought our carriage, and returned to the hotel in time to dress for dinner. I was determined to take one expedition into the country before leaving for the islands, so on the Saturday I started from Constant Spring Hotel with a friend by a tram, leaving shortly after six to catch the first train to Spanish

Town, from which place we intended to take a carriage to the Rio Cobre. This town, the capital of the Spaniards, was called San Jago de la Vega; it is not particularly interesting. The Governor's residence was here till quite recently. In the banqueting-hall and ball-room one may picture the scenes which took place in the days of West Indian prosperity at the King's House in Spanish Town. We found the most interesting object to be the cathedral, where lie interred many early Governors, their wives, and some of the first settlers of the island. The architecture is simple, though varied. The verger, who conducted us to the top of the tower and pointed out the principal objects, was interesting in the fact that he had been born there and evidently loved every stone of the place. He directed our gaze to one of the oldest epitaphs. It ran—

> "Here lyeth the body of Dame Elizabeth, the Wife of Sir Thomas Modyfort, Baronet, Governor of his Majesty's Island of Jamaica, who died the 12th of November 1668 being the 20th year of their happy wedded life."

A marble statue of Queen Victoria stands in the public Square, and bears the inscription—

VICTORIA
OF GREAT BRITAIN AND IRELAND
QUEEN
EMPRESS OF INDIA
AND OF JAMAICA SUPREME LADY
1837-1901.

We did not go to see the United Fruit Company's plantation of bananas, oranges and pines, but I believe it well repays a visit, so does the Cayman sugar estate, where some of the best rum is made.

We preferred to take a drive up the Rio Cobre of about nine miles. This is really beautiful; the road winds along the course of the river, and the luxuriant growth on either bank is simply wonderful to a person fresh from home and new to tropical scenery. Huge banana-trees, enormous clumps of bamboo, meet one at every turn in the road. We extracted a good deal of information from our driver, although we could not always understand him. Bare-legged women with skirts tucked up passed us with the inevitable yam-laden basket on their heads, crowned with the hat which was to cover the woolly hair of the lady when she set down her load; one or two begged for *quatties*, an old Spanish word still used and representing one penny halfpenny in our money. It is not often the natives beg of you, although they will turn round and tell you how much they love you! We had a delightful but very hot day, and did not get back till quite late in the evening. There was one more event which I have to record before closing these pages for a time on Jamaica. This was the opening of a new wing added during the last year to the hotel.

    Tourists, apparently, are beginning to make this island into a favourite winter resort, the consequence being that increased accommodation was needed. Elder, Dempster and Co., who own the hotel, were celebrating the event by giving a garden-party. Their agent, Mr Haggart, had arrived. The Governor was expected, and people were arriving in crowds, making a gay picture of the lawns in front of the hotel, where a West Indian band from one of the regiments was playing. It was nearly five o'clock when the gubernatorial party arrived. Their Excellencies were conducted over the new part of the building, afterwards to the new golf links, upon which Sir Augustus played the first round. The most important part of the programme consisted in his speech, in which he formally opened the new wing. He spoke ably, and congratulated the Company on their enterprising spirit, and hoped a new tide of success was about to float the island into a more prosperous condition. Her ladyship stood close by, as he spoke; so did the venerable, but tuft-hunting Delicia, so did the industrious Russian journalist, taking notes the while, but I looked in vain for persons of importance supporting their chief. I wondered where the influential residents, the representatives of the mercantile world, and government officials had betaken themselves to, and enquired of a well-known lady in Kingston the reason of their absence. It was the old story: they preferred to stay away. One felt sorry that things were so. However, the afternoon was very enjoyable. The hotel provided refreshments in the most generous and handsome way. Everyone present could only hope that Jamaica in the near future may be as flourishing as the most sanguine of her boomers could desire.

B. Pullen-Burry

CHAPTER IX

THE ROYAL MAIL COMPANY— THE "MUMPISH MELANCHOLY" OF JAMAICA

It was on the 2nd of December, 1902, that I left Kingston for my trip to some of the islands in the Caribbean Sea, in company with a couple of fellow-passengers who had journeyed out with me from England in the *Port Antonio*. In answer to my enquiries, the only feasible thing, apparently, to do was to travel by the Royal Mail Steam Packet Company as far as Trinidad, there to be transshipped into a smaller steamer of that Company, which takes cargo and distributes the English mails fortnightly, in connection with the outcoming steamers from Southampton as far as the Danish island of St Thomas. To my disappointment, I learnt that I should have to return by the same route to Jamaica, instead of making a circuit and visiting Porto Rico, as I had hoped to do.

No regular communication exists between St Thomas and Jamaica excepting that of the Royal Mail Company, although I might have accomplished what I desired had I remained on at St Thomas, and taken the first chance steamer, sloop, or schooner, bound for Porto Rico, and so on to Jamaica. But I felt this was too indefinite and scarcely good enough, St Thomas being neither very remarkable nor possessing good accommodation. As it turned out, I was not sorry to revisit most of the islands, especially those of Martinique and St Vincent, Dominica and St Lucia, the two latter being by far the most beautiful; and I was glad to have a chance of seeing the volcanoes twice over to impress my memory with their awe-inspiring and fearful aspect.

It is well to know what to do and what not to do in the West Indies. Although many, like myself, would be naturally desirous to see Nature active in her volcanic haunts—for, apparently, as Jamaica is the natural habitat of the sugar-cane, so the Caribbean Sea is specially marked out for these fiery outpourings of Vulcan—I cannot recommend them to follow in my footsteps, if they value comfort in the smallest degree.

In my case it was Hobson's choice. At the office of the Royal Mail Company at Kingston there was a vague talk of tourist ships, later on, being specially run to do this trip; but as no date could be given of their probable departure, or certainty entertained as to whether they would run at all, I resolved to travel by the s.s. *Para*. The cost of my ticket was £24; this was at the rate of £1 a day, for I expected to be in Jamaica again before the close of 1902. At the back of this ticket was written "with tourist privileges." What those were I have yet to learn, for a more uncomfortable journey I never experienced than the fortnight I spent in this Company's steamer, the *E——*. You are unfailingly reminded by its officers that the R.M.S. was incorporated by Royal Charter 1839, and since then has had the monopoly of trade with the West Indies, and you as often mentally wonder why they are letting such a good thing slip through incompetent management. The very mention, even, of the Direct Company's name has, in some instances on board these steamers, been like a red rag to a bull.

Since, however, I made my journey to the volcanoes a new

manager has come upon the scene. Things are changing, and one is glad to hear of a regular overhauling of both offices at home and ships at sea.

Personally, I never heard so much grumbling at sea in my life as I have from passengers travelling in these regions. Perhaps the heat makes them unwarrantably irritable. The prohibitive charges on freight have for years operated as the great hindrance to the development of the resources of the islands. Indeed, in the interests of the Company, it is well that things are being looked into.

The late manager of the Royal Mail Company was an admiral of the British navy, of whom many stories are afloat, showing that he was fearfully and wonderfully made to hold such an important post. Probably the man was an expert on shipbuilding and seamanship; most likely there his qualifications ended. For a purely mercantile undertaking, one cannot suppose a retired admiral would possess sufficient commercial experience to warrant his efficiency as manager. My own knowledge of naval men would incline me to the belief that they would rather laugh to scorn all suggestions of financial retrenchment.

There may be, however, some adventurous spirits, who, in the face of discomfort, will want once in their lives to visit these historical islands, and, however they go, they must trans-ship at Trinidad or Barbadoes, as I did, into the smaller ships of this Company. Of course they can go by Dr Lunn's tourist parties, but everybody does not care to visit places in gangs.

The *Para* is a comfortable, steady ship, notwithstanding her venerable age. The *Trent*, with her sister-ship the *Tagus*, are very handsomely appointed vessels of modern construction, carrying good cooks.

We had a lovely run in the *Para* from Kingston to Trinidad; it took three days. We saw no land until we approached the Bocas, the two entrances into the Gulf of Paria, the Dragon's Mouth, and the Serpent's Mouth. This gulf is a shallow lake, and forms a harbour of enormous size, where ships of every nation, almost, ride at anchor.

We arrived at sunset, and the sky was a lovely rosy pink. The purple mountains of the island ranges, nearly two thousand feet high, divided the vast expanse of the heavens from the crimson waters of the harbour, lazily lapping the quay-sides of Port of Spain. Trinidad, discovered also by Columbus, is very hot and very prosperous. It belonged to the Spaniards till 1797, since which time it has belonged to us. Cocoa plantations flourish, and the Lake of Pitch is—and, I presume, will be for years to come—a magnificent source of never-failing wealth. From it large quantities of asphaltum are taken and exported.

Charles Kingsley raves over this home of tropical verdure, but I am not a naturalist, nor do I stay at Government Houses.

I found Trinidad the most trying place of any in the West Indies. The mosquitoes are positively unbearable; no part of your person is sacred from their nomadic and predatory excursions. Kickshaws, in the way of lace-trimmed parasols, will not suffice you for the sun, however festive the occasion may be to call forth dainty sunshades. Be advised in time: fling appearances to the four winds of heaven, sally forth in the largest of shady hats, carry the largest umbrella you can find, but go not into the streets shopping, or otherwise, without a waterproof, for the rains are characterised by a ferocity in their down-pouring unknown in other climes. Take also a fan to withstand the heat, which is ever present, and a never-ceasing hindrance to personal enjoyment.

Everybody drives the smallest distances, but there are times when, encumbered with these three indispensable articles in overpowering heat (you may perhaps have to traverse a hundred yards, as from the landing-quay to the Royal Mail Company's Offices) when life is not worth living, unless you are a person of exceptionable amiability.

Most of the visitors to Port of Spain contented themselves with lolling round on "rockers" on the verandah of the largest hotel, called Queen's Park Hotel, where the rooms are airy and spacious, but the food is not always to be trusted. It looks out on to the savannah, a circular, fairly level tract of grass, round which an electric tram whirls the inhabitants of an evening for a breath of fresh air.

What really interested me was the beautiful Botanical Garden, containing a library and fine herbarium. Here, indeed, the wonderful parasitical growth on leviathan trees is simply astounding. If you wish to obtain orchids and other rare botanical plants apply to the Superintendent. I went twice with friends to these gardens; each time I was quite fascinated in watching the "parasol" ants hurrying to and fro in countless well-worn tracks, sometimes crossing our path, sometimes alongside of us carrying pieces of green leaf, frequently as large as a shilling. It was quite a green procession; they each kept to their appointed side of the path, those who had deposited their green burdens returning on the other side in search of fresh "parasols." Policemen regulating traffic in our London streets could not have done the thing in better style. If the hot, moist heat made us resemble the sluggard, we had not far to go to learn industry from these skurrying little insects, whose ways are past finding out. We were cautioned not to try to pursue their tracks, which wind incredibly long distances among the undergrowth on either side of the paths, scorpions being not infrequently met with.

On the voyage to Trinidad I met some Cambridge acquaintances, people who had been on the *Para* throughout the voyage from England. They had landed both at Cartagena and at Colon, on the coast of Central America, and gave graphic accounts of the horrors of the civil war which has raged in Columbia these three years past. They were at Colon before peace was concluded, and it was pitiable to hear of the condition of the soldiers, mostly boys of enfeebled physique and stunted growth, scarcely strong enough to carry the old-fashioned guns given them. All looked starved, with an expression of utter despair imprinted on their woebegone countenances. A lady told me she collected bread from the ships and handed it to them on the quay. The wretched youths fought over it as dogs for a bone; but a frozen sheep was given to them from one of the vessels lying alongside, which they tore into pieces amongst themselves, eating it raw.

Their women followed them to war; without their inciting them to fight, I am told, the Columbians would scarcely attempt to defend themselves. But when once roused, they fight like diminutive devils! The women too, on one occasion, rushed a bridge, and took it during the last war. The most horrible thing I heard about them was that they had no ambulance, and no doctors!

Whilst I was in the Caribbean Sea, Hayti was in a disturbed state, Cuba in a transitional condition, erupting volcanoes destroying whole cities, as at Martinique and in Guatemala. The Columbian Republic was resting out of sheer exhaustion from further civil warfare, whilst her neighbour Venezuela was in the throes of political revolution, figuratively torn in pieces by her rival presidents and her offended European debtors. Possibly times in the West Indies are bad for those who have put their trust in sugar, but life and property are safe under British rule. No one need starve unless he be irredeemably idle. If big fortunes are no longer attainable, still there is no need for the "mumpish melancholy," so well described by the Hon. S. Ollivier, Acting-Governor of Jamaica. He says: "I have observed that, as a people, we have a habit of being rather sorry for ourselves. We have not the cheerfulness of the Barbadian. On the other hand, our depression makes us mumpish and melancholy rather than vicious and violent. We overdo our talk of depression, we overdo our talk of the extravagancies of the Government, of the superfluity of our public officials. Our visitors take for public gospel what we promulgate for private consumption."

To return to my journey to Trinidad on the *Para*. About thirty-five persons belonging to an English Opera Company were journeying to Trinidad. They had previously been playing in Kingston, and had been not only to all our colonies, but recently had been touring up the western coast of South America. I gathered they had had splendid houses in most of the large towns, such as Valparaiso, Santiago, and Lima, though the artistes with whom I conversed declared that the heat and the indifferent food they had had put before them, though taken to the best hotels, had been most trying to their health. The poor things looked terribly worn, and evidently made the most of the rest of the three days' sea-voyage before performing again at Port of Spain. They had about thirty plays in their *repertoire*, which included all the best known pieces and the most popular, such as *The Geisha*, *The Shop Girl*, etc. I met them on the return journey a fortnight later, returning *viâ* Kingston *en route* for Bermuda, Halifax, Nova Scotia, and St John's, Newfoundland. I mention having met these strolling players, because I think that many of one's friends in the British Isles would have no notion that the inhabitants of such distant countries had an opportunity of ever becoming acquainted with the well-known airs of Sullivan and other popular composers. Without belittling or depreciating our well-meaning but somewhat ignorant dwellers at home, it is well for us to wake up from insular habits of thinking, and to discover that outside our particular zone of influence civilised life is throbbing. In every sphere of labour men are searching for better methods, and, as in America, are not satisfied until they get them. We need to keep our eyes open if we would not lose our place in the world's history! Conservatism such as ours does not reign in regions where dollars are plentiful, and where men are not fettered by the traditions of the past.

It was late on Friday night, 5th December, when we were trans-shipped into the inter-colonial boat, the *E——*.

I have previously stated that Barbadoes has hitherto been the meeting-place of the outcoming steamer and of the three smaller ships, whose mission it is to distribute the mails on three distinct routes.

The *E——* was bound for the islands as far as St Thomas, the *Solent* for La Guayra on the Venezuelan Coast, whilst the third steamer was setting off for Grenada and Tobago.

CHAPTER X

THE CUISINE OF THE E——.– THE ROMAN CATHOLIC BISHOP OF DOMINICA

I do not intend to relate my experiences day by day from the time that I joined the Royal Mail Company's steamship *E——*, but it behoves me to explain once more to those who would like to take this trip, that unless they can possess their souls in patience, and are in the best of health, they may find more discomfort than gain, more pain than profit in this so-called pleasure trip. Of course I may have had the ill-luck to strike a ship (please excuse the Yankeeism, but at Mandeville where I am writing, we are being invaded by Americans, whose object in life seems to me to be the erection of twenty-three storied sky-scrapers) where the captain, the purser, and the steward were suffering from a temporary loss of the sense of taste, either individually or collectively. The cook was a black, and from the culinary incapacity of the sons of Ham may I, in the future, mercifully be delivered! Of all the inappetising-looking viands, of all the nauseous compounds, the component parts of which you could not even guess at, ever set before defenceless travellers, favoured specially with tourists' privileges, those we had would take the cake. The first few days the food was incredibly bad, the meat uneatable, sometimes putrid, the bread mouldy, the butter rancid, the bananas rotten, and the oranges unripe! This was whilst we were in port. Things improved somewhat when we were once away from Trinidad. We certainly had better fruit and delicious pines from Antigua, but the food was often sent away untouched, for the cooking was of the very vilest description possible. This, though bad enough, was not the only discomfort endured in that ever-memorable voyage.

Of course the heat and the mosquitoes were inevitable. Fortunately the cleanliness of one's cabin was a feature to be noted; also the advantage of having it to oneself was a thing to be thankful for; but the memory of the hot, weary, sleepless nights I endured from the noise and rattling winches at work, hoisting up and taking on cargo, which went on at all the ports we touched on our way going up to St Thomas, haunts me yet. Other ships of a less obsolete type are providentially provided with hydraulic cranes to do this work, but I have yet to learn that this particular Company favours any but old-fashioned methods of working. This frightful noise went on over my head; outside my cabin door the niggers in the hold bawled to those working the hoisting or lowering apparatus, as the case might be, whilst the officers shouted down orders to them. There were three consecutive nights with more or less of this hideous din going on, when exhausted nature was demanding sleep. Anything more purgatorial could scarcely be conceived. I was ill for a week from these privileges. When we did have a night free from this pandemonium, the ship was being driven through the water at such a rate we were not allowed to have our port-holes open for fear of being semi-swamped—and this in the tropics! The stewardess was an enormously fat coloured woman of Barbadoes, much given to religion. She was a happy, good-natured body, but incapable of work. It was not pleasant to find yourself in a marble bath which apparently was never scrubbed out from one end of the year to the other.

A married couple, who had travelled to Jamaica on the *Port Antonio* and were also taking this trip, complained with just cause of the fare given us. In these islands fruit, at least, is cheap. On the evening of the 8th of December our dessert consisted of rotten oranges, ditto bananas, and nuts! I think the menu for breakfast on the 16th of December will remain a standing joke whenever we meet. The tempting dishes offered us were salt-fish, pork chops, and brains! I forget how the latter were served. After a sleepless night and in tropical heat, I need scarcely say that I did not partake of any. We went empty away mostly!

A lady passenger had also an experience which shows how very absurdly the regulations on these ships are adapted for tourists, or indeed for anybody wanting to see something of the islands we passed.

She was on deck at 7.30 A.M. one morning, when one of the ship's officers approached her, and informed her it was one of the rules that ladies should not appear on deck till breakfast-time. The lady is a daughter of a well-known judge, and her answer was given on judicial lines, to the effect that no mention of such regulation was on her passage ticket, and since she came to see the scenery, she intended every morning when there was land in sight to come up as early as she chose. She said later on to me: "Fancy passing La Soufrière, or any other equally interesting place for which you were enduring stifling heat, mosquitoes, sleepless nights, and bad food, and not allowed to be on deck to see it!"

This was the only mention made of their famous regulation; we never enquired whether it was a printed one, or an unwritten tradition of the Company.

From the accounts I have since heard from people coming out to the West Indies by the Royal Mail Company's tickets, advertised in the daily papers at £65 for sixty-five days, I am sure it is not generally understood that in these inter-colonial mail-boats passengers, whether tourists or persons having tickets with "tourist privileges" inscribed on them, like myself and Mr. and Mrs. S——, endure all the discomforts of cargo-boats, and, in addition, suffer from the restrictions of a mail service bound by contract to deliver and collect mails at certain times at certain places.

We never knew at what hour we should land at the different West Indian towns. It would have been an impossibility to order saddle horses, or carriages, to be in readiness for us had we desired them, nor could we ever ascertain with any degree of reliability how long we should stay at any given place until we got there; all was uncertain, indefinite. The mails, naturally, were the first consideration; what cargo to discharge, or to ship, was the next; and last of all, the convenience of the passengers. I give this as my own personal experience—I only hope other people have fared better! If there was any place like Martinique, for instance, which we particularly wanted to see, we invariably arrived when it was dark. Fortunately, on the return journey one was in some cases able to see towns one had missed in this way.

At the Royal Mail Company's office at Kingston, when I made my arrangements to travel by their ships, I was informed in flowing language what a beautiful cruise it was to the islands, and that I should never regret it! It *was* beautiful, and if I shall never regret having made it, I certainly shall never forget it. I consider the journey from Trinidad up to St. Thomas a bad one if business compels one to make it; as a tourist trip, and therefore a pleasure trip, it is quite unworthy of the name, especially in these days when the latter are so skilfully and so ably arranged and conducted by people who really consider their *clientèle*. Having had the experience, I have not failed to warn people, especially those who are not strong, of its discomfort and disadvantages!

The best way for those who have time and leisure to see the northern group of islands is to stay at Dominica, where there are frequently very fair opportunities of visiting the contiguous islands. It is a lovely, mountainous, and picturesque island. There are, I was told by a gentleman who had stayed in them, very comfortable lodgings to be had, kept by an Englishwoman; and this, he said, was better than putting up at the small hotel, where the food was not so reliable. I have also met people who have stayed for weeks in this island and have never found it dull. For men there is shooting and fishing in the rivers. An introduction by a member of the club should be obtained, for there are golf links, and, as in all hot countries, plenty of tennis.

The chief charm of life in Dominica consists in the exquisite rides amongst the mountains where there are sulphur springs, a boiling lake, and waterfalls to be visited. I have on a previous page alluded to the very promising condition of things in Dominica, and I have also mentioned that limes and cocoa are its principal exports. I had time to take a lovely walk in the valley of the Roseau, just at the back of the town, and was much impressed by the loveliness of the scenery, as well as with the prosperous-looking plantations on either side of the road. At the end of the valley a turn in the road exposed the peak called Morne Diablotin to view; it is 4750 feet, and the mountains are the highest in the Lesser Antilles.

On my return journey from St. Thomas no less a person than the Roman Catholic Bishop of Dominica, with two or three attendant priests, came on board at St Kitts. He was introduced to me, and told me quite a number of interesting things about the islanders. Some few Caribs, he said, remained still. I asked if his Church had many adherents in Dominica. "Ninety per cent.," he told me, adding that it had been a French possession longer than an English one.

The Bishop, who is a Belgian and not long consecrated, was a very chatty and amusing person; I admired his skilful tactics. Naturally he was somewhat prejudiced in favour of our late enemies, the Boers; but politics and religion he very wisely eschewed. I was amused at his ways. If he wanted his deck chair removed from one side of the deck to the other he always called his servant, or secretary—I could not tell in what capacity the man stood—to do it for him. Brother Boniface was the oddest-looking creature I ever saw. He was short, fair, and very much freckled, scant locks of sandy hair peeped out from under a very broad-brimmed black felt hat. His habit was black, and came to his boot tops, being confined round the middle of his shapeless body with a black shining belt. Between its irregular folds and the top of his boots, white stockings, which probably were knitted by a Belgian grandmother many years gone by, showed at intervals, their pristine whiteness being somewhat the worse for wear. A very large black stuff umbrella completed Brother Boniface's toilet. He was continually smiling, and his very large mouth looked always ready for a good meal. As we approached Dominica the mountains were veiled in mists, and everything had to give way for the drenching torrential rain which poured on to the deck. I was standing close by the Bishop, and admired the artistic effects of the mist-wreathed mountainous coast.

"I prefer to have them so," I said, pointing to the mountains. "There are some things which are best left undefined, indefinite, mysterious. Don't you think so, Monseigneur?" I looked round at him.

He looked meaningly at me—I fancy he knew I was secretly thinking of the very definite statements of the Romish Church—and then said: "Do as you suggested the other day. Come and spend a month on the island."

"I should very much like to do so," I answered simply.

"Our people are very good—you don't think they can be?" he asked, in a quick way which seems natural to him.

"Oh yes, I do," was my reply; "I don't see how they can fail to be so with such a good bishop." And there our conversation and short acquaintance ended.

B. Pullen-Burry

CHAPTER XI
DR GRAY ON YELLOW FEVER— MONT PELÉE—THE RED CARIBS OF DOMINICA

Since my object in putting pen to paper is to recount my Jamaican experiences of the winter of 1902-3, it will not be fitting, and it might be monotonous, to describe each island as we came to it. Suffice it to say that as Trinidad is the best off of the British possessions in the Caribbean Sea, so Antigua is the poorest; it has even been necessary to cut down the official salaries. The failure of sugar is the reason of its poverty. The Governor of the Leeward Islands resides at Antigua. We stood 4 miles out from St John's, the chief town of that island, where heavy seas made the landing most difficult. There was a good deal of cargo to be left at this place, and as we came up the companion after dinner that evening, it was quite a sight to see the tall masts and sails of the lighters alongside, rolling in the dim light, as well as to see huge cases roped together poised in the air, waiting for the right moment when the lighter rose on a high wave to drop as gently as circumstances permitted. On the other side passengers were also waiting for the right moment to land from the steam-tug. Some amusing "deckers" joined the ship at this port; these answer to our steerage passengers. I saw a newly-married couple of blacks come on board, both as well dressed as white people of a corresponding class at home. The woman in white piqué, starched as they only can starch in the West Indies, wearing a much-beflowered white hat, and holding an enormous bunch of flowers. Her newly-made husband wore an immaculate suit of grey, and carried the luggage, consisting of one chair and two basins!

Deckers have no quarters below stairs. They remain all night under an awning, but as their journeys are generally from port to port, their lot is not a hard one. We had brought along with us a pale-faced Irish curate, who was met by the Bishop of Antigua.

From St Kitts a delicate-looking girl came on board, the daughter of a sugar-planter, whose family had been settled some generations there. She amused me by her readiness to drink cocktails at all hours of the day; in fact, she gave me to understand that it was quite customary with many West Indian ladies to drink one before dinner as an appetiser. It is quite true that the enervating climate is most exhausting. Personally, I should be sorry to have to coax a jaded appetite in this way.

We had an interesting personage with us at one time on the *E——*, a tall, dark-browed, silent, narrow-chested Spaniard, who smoked cigarettes all day. He was suffering from *berri-berri*, and people said he was the ex-president of a small republic called Acre, which has quite recently been a source of contention between the governments of Brazil and Bolivia. It owes its existence to Sir Martin Conway, of exploring fame, who discovered its resources, and pointed them out to some enterprising Americans. This tiny republic is far up on the banks of the Amazon. Report said that before leaving the scene of his presidency he had feathered his nest, his gains being safely invested in European securities, but so much mystery lies around the rise and fall of South American presidents, that one may unconsciously fall into error in giving too much credence to reports which spread too easily when they concern noteworthy individuals.

One other personage, whose scientific knowledge interested me greatly, was a Colonial assistant-surgeon from Castries, the chief town of St Lucia. He was returning to England, having just been offered a more advanced appointment in our West African possessions. He gave me a paper to read, which he had drawn up on the conveyance of disease by mosquitoes, in which he declared: "It is no longer a theory, but an established fact, that Malaria and Yellow Fever are conveyed from the sick to the healthy by mosquitoes." He further explained many interesting experiments which have been made with "infected mosquitoes," which, he stated, "ought to convince the most sceptical that yellow fever (and other diseases) is carried by mosquitoes." The result of the establishment of this theory resolves itself into "the destruction of the mosquitoes which carry them (parasites), and of their breeding-places." These latter he describes to be such places as stagnant swamps and offensive puddles and pools. It is interesting also to know that the Military Governor of Havana, General Leonard Wood, issued instructions for the method of disinfection for yellow fever based on this theory, and the effect of this change is, that this particular disease has been stamped out of Havana in less than ten months, and the city which has been the home of yellow fever since 1762 can now rank as a healthy city of the world. "Finally," he wrote, "the complete control over the spread of yellow fever that the Sanitary Department of Havana has obtained this year, by the enforcement of prophylactic measures that are based solely on the doctrine of the transmission of yellow fever by the mosquito, goes very far to prove that there is no other channel of communication of the disease. These results have been obtained by the systematic destruction of mosquitoes in every house where a case presented itself. If this success is interrupted, the responsibility must fall upon the physician who conceals a case of the disease." Evidently the splendid results of the Cuban campaign against mosquitoes has exceeded the expectations of the most sanguine, and one may hope in a few years this disease, which is the scourge of the Brazils and many tropical countries, will be relegated to the history of the past.

When I contemplated taking the trip to the islands it was naturally my hope to see Mont Pelée in action, nor was I entirely disappointed. On the route up to St Thomas the mountain was partially enveloped in the densest donas of smoke, but returning, we went as near the shore as was prudent. The mountain then was covered in impenetrable clouds of smoke. It was a moonlight night and the effect was grand, but weird in the extreme; lightning at intervals was illuminating the sky to the north, but no rain fell. Presently, as we approached nearer, we smelt sulphur and felt dust in our faces, together with warm currents of air. We kept our eyes fixed on the crater, or, to speak more correctly, at the spot where we supposed it to be. Nor were we disappointed, for we saw a stream of "living fire" leap from under the thick concealing smoke and race down the mountain-side in a serpentine track. We did not see it plunge into the sea, but the officer on the bridge got a sight of it. He told us afterwards that it had taken exactly ten minutes for this fiery torrent to travel five miles, which was the distance the sea lay from the old crater. The whole aspect was terrifying. One felt one did not care for a nearer acquaintance with a burning mountain.

We did not land at St Pierre to see the ruins; for that you require a French permission. We saw where they lay, and a tiny light glimmered close down towards the water's-edge, which probably belonged to the craft which the professor at the Observatory has ready for escape at the first symptom of danger. St Pierre must have been one of the most important towns in the West Indies. It was the most famous town of Martinique, and contained 25,000 persons. It used to be the port of call of the Royal Mail; the steamers go now to Port of France, between which and St Pierre a beautiful road, bordered with woods, formed the favourite drive taken by visitors to the island. On either side are seen "giant ferns and huge parasites clinging to the branches of gigantic trees, the whole woven together by creepers of extraordinary grace. Suddenly the view opens out, and splendid points of vantage are reached whence one commands the eastern and western sides of the island; for this road, traced (whence its name Trace) for the most part by the Caribs almost always follows the ridge of the mountains."

In disembarking at St Pierre one was faced by the Place Bertin; on one side stood a round tower serving as a semaphore, having a red light visible for 9 miles, opposite stood the Chamber of Commerce. The town possessed two banks, a seminary, a theatre, a military hospital, rum factories and a beautiful Botanical Garden with quantities of native and exotic plants, waterfalls, and a miniature lake with three islets called respectively, Martinique, Dominica, and Guadeloupe, because their shapes were similar to these islands. Life was luxurious at this French colonial town; every house had its bath-room, there was an excellent hydropathic institution, food was abundant and cheap. Whether or no there was any truth in the report that this city was famed for its wickedness, I am not able to say. St Pierre, I know, was considered by many to be a modern Gomorrah, and piously-disposed people regarded its extinction as the righteous judgment of an indignant Deity. I will only refer my readers on this head to a story of what went on at St Pierre, Good Friday afternoon last (1902), as given in an article in *The Fortnightly* of October 1902, entitled "A few Facts concerning France." It appears that atheistical agitators went to the island preaching an anti-religious crusade, the outcome of which was on that Good Friday afternoon a procession paraded the streets of St Pierre, hooting and blaspheming. In the midst of this gathering of human scum was held aloft, on a cross, a pig, crucified alive. Its head was adorned with wreaths of flowers, and the crowd mockingly aped its dying wriggles. To put a climax to their folly, in a mad rush of hatred towards all things sacred they marched up the slopes of Mont Pelée to a spot where a Calvary stood, and was seen far and wide in the island landscape. This they tore down, flinging the crucifix into the crater, with shouts of "Go to hell, from whence thou camest!" I met a very charming French priest, who had, by his own exertions, built a church in one of the parishes of Dominica; I believe it was called Soufrière. I asked him concerning the truth of this story. He had heard of it, but—and he lifted up his hands in holy horror at the very mention of the wickedness of St Pierre—he was not able to confirm it, though he considered it more than likely to be true. In Mr George Kennan's book, which describes the tragedy of Pelée, an interesting incident is recorded. On the eve of the catastrophe a local newspaper called *Les Colonies* deprecated the panic which had been caused by previous heavy detonating explosions and the appearance of incandescent matter at the summit-fissure, in consequence of which many persons left for different parts of the island. "Mont Pelée is no more to be feared by St Pierre than Vesuvius is feared by Naples," said this newspaper. Captain Leboffe, the skipper of the Italian barque, *Orsolina*, which was in the harbour loading with sugar for Havre, thought differently. He went to the shippers, told them he did not consider the roadstead safe, and gave notice that he should sail for Havre immediately.

"But," said they, "you can't go yet; you have not got aboard half the cargo."

The captain, however, declared he should sail rather than risk remaining there. The shippers angrily explained that the mountain was not dangerous, since it had once before thrown out ashes and smoke in the same way.

"If Vesuvius looked as your volcano does this morning, I'd get out of Naples, and I am going to get out of here," said he. The shippers told him if he sailed without permission and without clearance papers he would be arrested on reaching Havre.

"All right," imperturbably he replied; "I'll take my chance of arrest, but I won't take any chances on that volcano. I'm going to get my anchor up, and make sail just as soon as I get aboard." And he went away.

The shippers sent two Customs officers to the barque, with instructions to prevent her leaving. The captain, however, addressed them as follows: "Gentlemen, I sail from this port in less than an hour. If you want to go ashore, now is your time to leave. If you stay, I shall take you to France."

When the sails were loosed, and the crew began to heave up anchor, the Customs officers hailed a passing boat and went ashore, threatening the captain with all the penalties of the law.

Twenty-four hours later St Pierre, with all its inhabitants, was wiped for ever out of the book of the living, but the barque *Orsolina* was speeding on her way to sunny France.

La Soufrière at St Vincent was awful in the desolation which the late eruption has produced; the line of demarcation was strictly defined between the green verdure of the country which had not suffered from devastating showers of dust and lava, and that which had been subjected to the outpourings from the crater. Puffs of white smoke here and there announced the neighbourhood of hot sulphur springs.

The inhabitants of Montserrat also lie under the shadow of a volcanic mountain; just above their little town is a crater which, like Pelée, may one day serve as a vent to the fires beneath. Temporary shelter at one corner of the island has been prepared for an emergency of this kind. Meanwhile, the islanders busy themselves very philosophically with the cultivation of limes, an industry which seems to be fairly remunerative. The speech of the people here is still said to recall the brogue of the Irishmen sent out by Oliver Cromwell.

I think one of the most interesting of the smaller islands we saw, but did not touch at, was the little Dutch island of Saba. Here a few hundred thrifty Hollanders inhabit an extinct crater several hundreds of feet above the waters of the Caribbean Sea; they reach their homes by means of ladders hanging from the cliffs. Curious to relate, in their isolated eyrie they build many of the schooners which ply locally from island to island. The ships are let down by ropes, and navigated by these extraordinary islanders, who are considered the ablest sailors in those waters.

It was interesting to find ourselves once more at Trinidad, for events on the Venezuelan coast had progressed since we had been away. We found ourselves riding at anchor within a few hundred yards of the flagship of our West Indian Squadron; other British warships were beside her, and not far away the captured fleet of Venezuela. The crews and men had been sent home. Of course Germany was represented, but America was there in full force to support the Munro policy, in the menacing form of four great warships, which lay motionless on the green waters of the Gulf of Paria. The blockade of the Orinoco had begun, and we met fugitives from the mainland at the hotel on shore, who seemed to have passed through lively times. I spent Christmas Day on the good ship *Trent*, belonging to the Royal Mail Service, where we were splendidly entertained, and the next morning at an early hour I found myself once more in Kingston.

I feel, however, I cannot bring my account, brief though it is, of what proved to be a very interesting trip, to a close, without some mention of that almost extinct race, the Caribs.

In a Jamaican newspaper an interesting report appears, written by Mr Hesketh Bell, who probably is the best authority living on the subject of the aborigines of the West Indies. He says: "The reserve set apart for the St Vincent Caribs was recently raked by the fire from the Soufrière. But these are Black Caribs, who, through long admixture of negro blood, have lost all the distinguishing traits of the aboriginal tribe. There still exists, however, in Dominica a handful of full-blooded Red Caribs, the last survivors of their race." Mr Bell, who is the Administrator of the last-named island, then alludes to the pre-Columbian tradition when fleets of canoes overran the Windward and Leeward Islands exterminating the males, but preserving the women of the milder Arawak nation. The latter handed down for many generations from mother to daughter their original tongue. He further says: "Whatever its origin, the Carib type, even in the remnant that survive to-day, shows an unmistakably Mongolian character, and it would be hard to distinguish a Carib from a Chinese or Tartar child." The Caribs were inveterate cannibals. Defoe, it is believed, placed the scene of his romance in Tobago, and the wild man Friday was presumably one of a hapless lot of Arawaks whom a party had captured, and were probably carrying north for the delectation of the tribe.

The Caribs, says Davis, after having tasted the flesh of all nations, pronounced the French the most delicate, and the Spaniards the hardest of digestion. Laborde interviewed a Carib who "beguiled the tedium of his journey by gnawing the remains of a boiled human foot"; he told the priest that he only ate Arawaks, "Christians gave him stomachache."

The Administrator goes on to describe how years of peace and protection have completely metamorphosed the Carib, and have arrested almost at the last gasp the extinction of this interesting remnant of one of the world's aboriginal races. Instead of a bloodthirsty, man-eating savage the Carib is now as law-abiding and mild a subject as any the King has. "He no longer paints crimson circles of roucou round his eyes and stripes of black and white over his body, but on high days and holidays he wears a tall hat and a black coat; instead of yelling round a sacrificial stone, the Carib of to-day goes to confession to the parish priest, and tells his beads with edifying fervour." The Carib Reserve at Dominica numbers nearly 400 members, probably 120 only are full-blooded. Out of 78 school-children, 26 are described by Mr Bell to have pure blood in them; their chief characteristics are bright, intelligent expressions, oblique eyes, straight hair, rather coarse, of a beautiful blue-black, the complexion varying from brown to a pinkish-yellow. Their chief claims to be of pure blood. He settles petty disputes. Ogiste, his little granddaughter, is evidently the last of his dynasty. She is more negro than Carib, according to the Administrator, and the Salic law prevails in the Carib Reserve.

CHAPTER XII

DRIVES AND COUNTRY LIFE AT MANDEVILLE—NEGROES AND FUNERAL CUSTOMS

It was on Boxing Day 1902, that I returned to Jamaica, the *Trent* arriving at Kingston at 7 A.M. enabled me to catch the morning train for Mandeville.

I breakfasted with friends at Myrtle Bank Hotel, was delighted to find a number of letters awaiting me at the post-office. I then betook myself at ten o'clock that morning to the railway station. These are, naturally, somewhat primitive; the trains, too, are not noted for their punctuality, they are known to break down occasionally, which is rather trying to the temper. I speak from sad experience. Still one remembers, if things are not up to date, that one is not in the most flourishing of the British Colonies.

In view of the late depression of trade, it strikes me, as it does nearly everybody I have met who considers the subject at all, that a large proportion of the island revenue goes to support a very expensive gubernatorial machinery which constitutes the government of this country.

When sugar was £70 instead of £5 a ton, when 100 lbs. of coffee fetched 80s. instead of 20s., when the wealth of the West

Indian planter was proverbial, the salaries of the officials were not disproportionate.

The prosperity of those days will never probably revisit this island, but the salaries are likely to remain at their present high figure. One hears much animadversion and grumbling on this subject from the better-class inhabitants of Jamaica. The Colonial Secretary, say they, might well have another thousand per annum in addition to his present stipend, if that would ensure so efficient and capable a man for that post as the present occupant; but it is apparent to many that £5000 a year, with a fine house to live in, wines and spirits free of duty, does not guarantee to the island either acceptable or fitting representatives of royalty.

At the same time, the stability and justice of the present government is fully appreciated by the inhabitants as well as by those Americans who have large financial interests, such as the Fruit Companies in Jamaica. Justice is administered to the black very differently by the present legislature than formerly. In the country districts the overseers who had to send to the absentee landlords annual sums from their estates invariably mulcted the negro of his pay to make up the deficit.

The information which Whittaker's Almanac supplies, under the head of Jamaica, will give to the reader an idea of how large and how expensive is the staff of officials who are employed in the government. The Government Handbook of Jamaica will give details as to the expenditure of the yearly revenue.

ROAD NEAR KINGSTON.

In 1900-1901 this amounted to £760,387. The expenditure of the same year was £763,902. I have heard it said that if you cut down the official incomes you won't get the right men, and that the Jamaicans would not like to be considered, or to rate themselves, a third-rate colony. If that be so, all one can say is, that they must pay for their pride. A government official, who worked hard for something under £400 a year, told me he thought that Englishmen would not live year after year in such an enervating climate unless the pay was good. He had been six years out here; his work was hard and unremitting, and he had not even left the island for a holiday in all that time. When he came to Jamaica he was an athlete, now he could scarcely run a quarter of a mile. Thus there are two sides to every question!

Soon after leaving Kingston we passed through swamps covered with mangroves, then through a thousand acres of level land quite recently irrigated and brought into cultivation. The climate here is hot, and specially suited to the growth of bananas. Since the days of sugar failure this has been a remunerative industry. Eleven years ago, about thirty bunches of bananas were imported into England. In 1901, 3,000,000 came from the Canaries and 450,000 from Jamaica. The revenue of the island for the first five months of the financial year 1902, exceeded by £40,000 the receipts for the same period in the year previous, and, owing to the extension of the fruit trade, the financial outlook is more hopeful than it has been for years. Canada, so the local papers say, is looking forward to consignments of Jamaican bananas.

The fact of Elder, Dempster & Co. having combined with the United Fruit Company means a continual market open to the banana trade, both in Britain and in the United States. The latter is an American enterprise, having steamers running between the West Indies, Boston, New York, Philadelphia, and Baltimore. Sir Alfred Jones, who is the moving spirit of the Direct Line, is most generous in his dealings with this poverty-stricken island. He announced, some months ago, that the Line he represents (Elder, Dempster) would take, free of freight from Bristol, English stallions, bulls, and rams, for breeding purposes, the object being to improve the breeds of cattle, there being splendid grazing land in some parts of the island.

At a dinner given by the West Indian Club in London, 1st October 1902, Sir Alfred Jones, in referring to the position of the West Indies, said he thought there "had been too much complaining, the people should do what they could themselves to develop the island. There were many possibilities before them. The tourist traffic might be developed, and there were splendid opportunities for breeding horses and cattle. Mineral also afforded a possible field for expansion. The great thing for West Indians was not to sit down and think they had a grievance, but to get up and put their shoulders to the wheel." He also referred to the prosperous olden time when activity reigned in the cotton industry, and trusted to see a revival of it some day. He believed in the future of the island, deploring the ignorance still reigning in England regarding the West Indies.

One is somewhat amused here at the newspaper revelations. Great confidence in Mr Chamberlain is felt over the difficulties connected with the Sugar Convention, etc. One paragraph states that a good deal of literature is being circulated just now concerning the injustice of depriving the working man at home of his cheap sugar. "The best answer," says the paper to this, "is that the Trades Unions are dead against bounties, and ask that bounty-fed sugar should be denied access to this country altogether."

Rumours of discontent are also to be heard in this land to the effect that the chief trade goes to America and not to Britain. Local economists talk of the mother-country giving preferential tariffs to her colonies and dependencies, having learnt their lesson from no less a person than Mr Seddon, of New Zealand fame. They should have heard Judge Shaw's paper, read last September in the Section of Economics, at the British Association, Belfast, in which he strove to show how the law of commercial development meant the natural and inevitable selection of the nearest market, whatever code of tariffs prevailed, and instanced Canada's trade with the United States as an example of this. If the mother-country were to give to her colonies preferential trading facilities, it would disorganise all existing fiscal agreements with every Continental power, he said, and the price she would pay would be financial and commercial suicide. Since we are a nation of shopkeepers and traders, our teeming millions of workers must be fed as cheaply as possible.

After passing through the level lands of St Catherine's parish, the line gradually ascends, until at Williamsfield, the station for Mandeville, it is 1000 feet above sea-level. The scenery becomes broken and wild as you get among the hills; dry river beds in the rainy season are roaring torrents. There are in the island upwards of 114 streams finding their way to the sea, besides numerous tributaries, some streams being navigable. When I glanced around at the different stations we stopped at, I never saw a white face. Porus is about 10 miles from Mandeville, and a quaint, busy little town. J. A. Froude says no explanation is given in any handbook of this singular name, but he found that a Porus figured amongst the companions of Columbus! From this place the train crawled, squeaked, and groaned up to Williamsfield.

A drive of 5 miles brought me to The Grove, Mandeville, a very comfortable private hotel, where I spent some happy weeks, and from whence I took pen in hand to relate my experiences. The drive from the station was lovely; the ground here is red and the foliage very green, which makes the country most picturesque. It is one continual ascent through roads bordered and sheltered with waving bamboos, palms, orange-trees, cedars, and mangoes. Sometimes one caught sight of magnificent silk-cotton trees standing in lonely grandeur in the midst of a pasture. At last, turning a sharp corner, the horses clattered up a steep, stony hill, rushed me across what looked like a village green, my driver pulling them up with a jerk in front of Mrs England's verandah. Intending visitors to Mandeville cannot do better than trust themselves to the above lady's catering; the food is excellent, the house most healthily situated, and everything is done with a view to the guest's comfort. Mrs England has not been long in the island, but she has managed to learn how to deal with the black domestics very successfully.

This district of the Manchester Hills in which Mandeville lies, is the heart of the orange industry; unfortunately, the beautiful tangerine which abounds, as well as the other kinds, will not keep long enough for packing. These grow wild in the hills, and negro children sell them at the station, six for a *quatty*, *i.e.* 1½ d. I saw large wooden buildings at Williamsfield owned by fruit shippers, where fruit bought locally is sorted as to size, wrapped in paper, and packed in barrels or boxes. Some enterprising person might well start a marmalade factory with the thousands of rejected ones thrown away.

The climate of this little township is eminently cool and recuperative. In August, residents come from Kingston to escape the excessive heat. After Christmas, Americans visit the island to avoid the rigorous cold of New York and the northern states. As I write, there is no representative of the British flag but myself amongst the guests.

Across the green, or parade, as it is called, stands a fine County Court House. Opposite, at a distance of two hundred yards or so, the parish church is to be seen. Irregularly placed around this central patch of grass are several stores where most things are to be purchased, also a chemist's shop, and a room where a dentist and a lawyer seem to hold appointments with their clients on alternate days. The place boasts of an hotel and a club, but its chief attraction to me is its large market, which on Saturdays is quite interesting. I have visited it with Mrs England and her cook on two occasions, and am beginning to know the look of the numerous island vegetables before they are cooked. Small cultivators come many miles to this market, and the blacks strike one as being more prosperous and more respectful than those at Kingston. The women carrying their stock-in-trade in large baskets on their heads, with a fine hat generally perched on the top of that, step like "young panthers," and often walk 5 miles an hour. The men or boys bring the goods to sell in baskets on donkeys, and sleep in the market shelters, I have often seen pigs sitting quite comfortably in these baskets, and looking as if they enjoyed their ride. Besides vegetables, chickens and native tobacco, twined into rope at 3d. a yard, are sold here. Dark, mysterious-looking pats of sugar, made in the negro's pot, also find customers. I hear the blacks make a drink of the latter. There is a shed for those who sell meat, but the rest of them just squat on the pavement, chattering together like magpies.

The majority of the parishioners are small growers, renting five, ten, or twenty acres at £1 an acre. Oranges nearly always pay the rent. Where science and method prevail in knowing how best to fertilise the trees, the grower gets a better crop and larger fruit; he can pack his own oranges and get 50 per cent. more for them.

Mandeville strikes one as thoroughly English; there are lovely walks and drives in the neighbourhood. Several families have properties not far from the town; in fact there seems quite a pleasant society for miles round. There is a tennis-club, to which people drive in their buggies. One of the ladies makes tea, and although these people have lost much of late years over the decline of the sugar trade, they are certainly hospitable, courteous, and refined. This is a charming spot to recruit in after the heat of the lowlands. One can walk in the moonlight for miles without the smallest fear of anything unpleasant. I have done so with Mrs England's daughters, and nothing is more enjoyable. One can see the foliage against the sky so much clearer, and the shapes of the different trees thus become impressed upon one's memory.

After nine o'clock, except just in Mandeville itself, not a soul is to be seen in the lanes. I fancy the negro goes to roost betimes like the feathered tribe. Perhaps this is because of his hereditary and ingrained fear of the supernatural. He calls all ghostly visitants "duppies," and tells you he sees them sitting on the trees where your own visual organ fails to inform you of any living thing, or otherwise.

One night three or four of us had emerged from deep shadow into bright moonlight: our dresses were white. Wheels were heard behind us, and immediately after, a one-horsed conveyance with two people sitting in it appeared. As it approached out of the gloom, the figure nearest us sat huddled up holding a huge umbrella close over its head. My companions recognised the chaise as belonging to an old black proprietor. We thought he had taken us for "duppies," and returned to the hotel much amused; but we were informed that the umbrella was not to protect its owner from ghostly visitants, but to keep him from getting moon-struck.

One day I took a drive to a property some miles from here, where the family owned a good old Norman name, well known in some parts of England. They had been settled in their estate for one hundred and fifty years, had seen both good times and bad. The house in which I sat was really a beautiful two-storied building with verandahs both downstairs and upstairs; the drawing-room was of noble proportions, and Mrs G—— told me that the wood employed in the construction had all been cleared from their own estate, and consisted principally of mahogany, bullet-wood, and cedar. They were several miles from a town or a market, and nearly everything that came to table was produced on the property.

The negro shanties about here are not very large for the accommodation of the numerous members of a family. The Keswick delegate, Mr Meyer, drew attention to the narrow limits of these. It seems the blacks will not build additional buildings or better accommodation since they would be liable to increased taxation. Each little home is mostly provided with yams, a few banana-trees, and several orange-trees planted anywhere without any method.

I have only so far summoned up courage to enter one of them belonging to a coloured woman who takes in washing. She informed me she had four children, "two young gentlemen and two young ladies." It is amusing to hear the negresses say to each other, "Yes, ma'am," and a negro in the wordiest altercation never fails to address his opponent as "Sah!" The greatest contempt which a woman feels for another is expressed in the words, "You black niggah!" They only call each other black niggahs when further words fail to express their disgust. A negro proverb says, "Choose wife Saturday on Sunday." This means if she works well on Saturday—and that is the great market day here—she can be asked to marry on Sunday, their leisure day and time for "walking out."

I was curious as to the burial-place of the black population, for the few churchyards I had seen with their scattered graves seemed out of all proportion to the population of the island. One day when I was out for a drive I learnt from a very loquacious driver that his elderly relatives were buried in the backyard of the little home he called his own, "under de shadder, missus, of a big cedar-tree, dar dey lie buried."

This I found to be true; that owing to hot climate and the distance at which some of these dwellings lie, it is deemed expedient to allow them to bury their dead in their own little properties. Of course they have to duly notify the fact. I could not help thinking that this custom would facilitate any nefarious proceedings on the part of those who might be benefited by the death of an aged relative, but I was assured on good authority that very rarely has anything of the kind come to light.

The peasantry have a great horror of prison, and have a wholesome terror of the officers of the law. At the same time, they are very litigious, and amongst themselves are much given to argument.

For a person desirous of spending a quiet winter in a warm climate, where they would be able to get out-of-doors every day for a certainty, I can think of no better place than Mandeville for them to come to. The drives are really exquisite; I have been most of them, which are generally about 6 miles away, returning by different routes. Thus, Fairview is the home of the widow of a Moravian minister who lived fifty years here; the house is built on a commanding situation on a spur of the Manchester Hills, from which one sees the sea at Alligator Pond on the south coast of the island, 17 miles away, whilst stretching far off on the right, an extended vista of the Santa Cruz Mountains is to be obtained. Here on the horizon, 30 miles away, a large palm-tree is pointed out, and Malvern House, 30 miles from Mandeville, is known far and wide as a comfortable hotel. The salubrious air of the Santa Cruz Mountains is much recommended for lung complaints by the medical faculty. Another very popular drive is to a spot called Bel Retiro; this is in exactly the opposite direction and is also on the summit of a hill, where a house is in course of erection on the ruins of an old sugar mill. A grand view over Old Harbour in the distance, and the white houses of Porus below one's feet, dotted amongst the green trees with the Manchester Hills in the background, constitutes another very lovely scene.

One day we had a picnic to an untenanted house, from which there was a beautiful view. The verandah from the upper storey was converted into a dining-room for the occasion, and nothing more enjoyable can be imagined than taking one's lunch with such an exquisite picture to gaze upon. Everywhere, so far as the eye could see, was undulating ground covered with tropical foliage, lofty cotton-trees and stately palms waved over coffee plantations, and negro huts here and there dotted the landscape. The house where we lunched, with 100 acres, was to be sold; the owner wanted £1200 for it.

Life in this quiet Jamaican country town passes pleasantly by, notwithstanding its distance from the attractions of the "madding crowd." One day the shouts of joyous school-children announced the fact of a Sunday School treat. Hundreds of children were entertained in the Rectory fields, in much the same way as similar gatherings in England. Swings and cricket seemed most popular amongst the small blacks, whilst the little girls' conscious grandeur in well-starched clean frocks was quite apparent.

Another time the unusual ringing of the church bell awakened our curiosity; we learnt that it was for service before the Parochial Board of Manchester held its customary meetings. Mandeville also has its tragedies; whilst I was there we were all shocked to hear that the proprietor of the local hotel had shot himself, owing to embarrassed circumstances. This establishment is very badly situated. The management for some time past has been unsatisfactory, and few visitors have cared to put up there, preferring the boarding-houses in the place. Perhaps it is only in tropical countries that one realises what walking shadows we are—this poor fellow had eaten his breakfast a little after seven o'clock that morning—shot himself at eight, was taken to his grave at a little after five the same afternoon. It happened on a Saturday—Mandeville market day; crowds of people coming in from the country stayed over to witness the funeral. All that afternoon the grave, which was being dug, was surrounded by onlookers who, squatting round, watched the progress with a curious expression of fascinated and morbid interest on their dusky faces, reminding us forcibly of the way their ghoulish scavengers, the John Crows, large black native buzzards, sit upon the house-tops surveying from that elevated vantage-spot the ground below, where haply some spicy breakfast awaits them in the garbage line.

Nothing appeals so much to the "duppy"-ridden imagination of the black as everything connected with our transit from this world to the next. The correct thing is to be *laid out* in a suit of clean white ducks and white gloves; whilst the women, if they have it, are similarly arrayed in clean white attire, also with the needful gloves. I asked the reason of this almost universal practice amongst them, and was told it was to "rise up tidy on de reburrection mornin," and also that they should appear fitly dressed to "sit down at de marriage supper of de Lamb." They are quite familiar with this phraseology, which is current in the chapels, which are numerous all over Jamaica; and as their mental powers of assimilation and digestion scarcely touch the spiritual plane, the crudity and grotesqueness of their ideas of another life, mixed up as they are with their hereditary Obeah-worship and dread of "duppies," produces curious results. They mostly celebrate a death with a wake, especially in the country parts. A clergyman's wife living in the Blue Mountains told me of a man who was ill, and expected quite confidently to die. His wife bought provisions for the burial wake. The chickens, with their legs tied together, were hung upon the bough of a tree, plenty of yams were in readiness, and the savings of weeks past were represented in the shape of a bottle of rum; the white duck clothes waved in the breeze in the backyard, having been duly washed. Strange to say, the man recovered. "It was in de middle of de night, missus," he explained to the lady. "I got hungry, and I felt under de bed wher dey put a box of sweet biscuits; I eat one, and den I ate up de rest and got well."

This was a box of Huntley & Palmer's sweet biscuits, carefully stowed away for the wake, which had resuscitated the invalid. "No man can dead before his time," they say in the country parts, and evidently this man's time had not yet come.

It was with feelings of regret that I turned my back on this pretty English-looking spot, although I looked forward with interest to staying a short time on a pen with friends not very far away from Mandeville.

CHAPTER XIII

MY VISIT TO A PEN—ARAWAK REMAINS—LEGEND OF THE COTTON-TREE

Kingston, *March 1903.*—After passing Kendal, a place well known for its yearly agricultural shows, I stopped at a station called Balaclava, where my friend in her buggy met me. A drive of about two miles through very hilly country and across one or two bridges spanning one of the many rivers, or springs, which abound in this island, brought me to their property. A gate stood open, and we drove over a grassy track up to the house, which is one of the oldest in Jamaica, and called a "storm-house," because it was built after the great hurricane of 1722. I was afterwards introduced to an ancient black lady of some eighty summers, who remembered slave times. She had been on the estate, and had never lived elsewhere. The house, she said, had always been "just de same, missus," when she was a "picaninny and lived in de big niggah houses ovar dar," pointing towards the wooded hills which lay on my right. My hostess, Mrs M——, said their property had been bought some years before from a coloured family, a death having caused the estate to be sold. It comprised 1600 acres, and besides coffee, which was chiefly grown, logwood, pimento and bananas were cultivated. A river ran through it, and they had on the estate a very interesting cave, about a mile in length, if I cared to visit it. I naturally accepted the latter proposal, and as we could not drive anywhere the next day, the horses and carriage having been promised to some friends for the purposes of a funeral, it was arranged we should visit the cave. Mrs M—— I found to be a most charming hostess, desirous that I should see all there was to be seen in the neighbourhood.

The house reminded me very much of some old-fashioned houses I had seen in Spain the previous spring. It was a square one-storied building with a low, wide verandah running round two sides of it. The ground floor was taken up with storage-rooms, an overseer's room, and a school-room. Passages were built between thick stone walls for shelter in case of violent storms or hurricanes. A small portion of grass was fenced round about the house to prevent the turkeys, chickens, sheep and pigs from entering the enclosure. On passing through the wicket-gate of this I was conducted up a stone staircase across the piazza or verandah into the drawing-room which, with a sitting-room, ran the whole length of the front of the building. An open doorway, draped with lace curtains, led into a large dining-room, which occupied the central portion of the house. The bedrooms were built on either side, and the kitchen ran along the back of the house. This central high-roofed, cool, windowless room is the characteristic feature of most West Indian houses built in times past. The floors, generally of island cedar-wood, are polished to a nicety by the black servants, who sing as they work at them.

The family, which consisted of Mr and Mrs M——, their three sons and daughter, a girl of nine, with her governess, a tall, dark West Indian girl, the daughter of a neighbouring clergyman, sat down to dinner about six o'clock the evening of my arrival. We were waited on by two neatly-dressed maids, whose faces reminded one of Nubian blacking; they wore caps on their woolly hair and slippers on their feet.

Mrs M——, who is a clergyman's daughter, and her husband, the son of a British naval commander, belonging to a good old Cornish family, told me that they insisted upon their servants appearing suitably dressed in the house, however smartly they chose to attire themselves out-of-doors. They interested me very much in their conversation about the condition of the island and the amusing ways of the blacks.

Jamaica, they said, had certainly taken a turn for the better; and it is commonly said amongst business-men out here, that the island can never return to the state of depression caused by the failure of sugar. Fortunes are perhaps not to be made, but that a living is to be earned if people are industrious and ordinarily intelligent is conceded on all hands, and was a feature to be noted in the Archbishop's address to his people for the New Year.

That Dr Nuttall, who is known far and wide as a man of clear-sighted ability, both as an energetic organiser and able administrator, is also an admirable judge of economic and financial problems in these latitudes no better evidence is forthcoming than a study of the methods by which he has guided the barque of the Anglican Church through the stormy waters of Disestablishment. In spite of almost overwhelming difficulties and penury, he has established it on a far surer foundation than it ever boasted of before, for it has its roots now in the hearts of the people. It represents to-day the chosen religious expression of the most enlightened and educated classes in this island.

But although I cannot refrain from speaking of the conspicuous ability which has retrieved the position of Anglicanism during the last two decades, it is not because one depreciates, or would wish to undervalue, the self-denying labours of Wesleyan and other nonconformist ministers. Pitying the condition of "poor slaves" they came to Jamaica in the eighteenth century, and commenced their labours when the clergy of the Established Church were steeped in avarice, or in apathy. Here they live and labour on the merest pittances. I heard recently of a nonconformist minister whose income, all told, was not over £40 a year.

Since I intend to devote other pages to this subject, I will shorten my reflections on religious phases in Jamaica, and will only mention the way in which my friends were able to get a church built in this neighbourhood.

Mr M——, adding some practical training he had had in his youth to certain handy-man qualities, inherited perhaps from a sailor ancestry, superintended the whole of the undertaking when once the spot of ground was selected, whereon to build. He was both architect and builder. Many of the contributors, who could not give money, gave their labour and time. The ladies of the country-side devoted their energies to the cause, inciting and encouraging their black sisters to aid them. Appeals to their friends in England for help met with generous response, and a bazaar, or rather country *fête*, brought in a very satisfactory sum total. The cost of the erection of the church to which I was taken probably represents the smallest amount in Jamaica, for one of its size.

It is difficult for us at home with our various secular interests improving, or otherwise, to realise how, in the life of the country people of our colonies, removed from all these, religion, whether sham or real, plays an all-important part. Only by living in these out-of-the-way places does one at all appreciate this side of colonial life, and, having seen it, one feels that if the want of solid teaching is felt amongst the educated laity, it should be met by the best possible attainable. So far as my own powers of observation go, I incline to think that the emotional side of religion is not what is needed in Jamaica; they have had plenty of that sort of thing. What they ask for is a broad-minded, literary, practical theology, which can hold its own with the advancing science and democratic faddisms of these days, and this it is the duty of the English Church, to, my mind, to provide.

An interesting visitor to the house whilst I stayed at N—— was a local doctor, with antiquarian and artistic tastes. I learnt from him that there had been several finds in the island of prehistoric remains, consisting of kitchen-middens, refuse-heaps, or shell-mounds, near which various objects such as aboriginal pottery, fish-bones, and those of the Indian coney had been discovered. The locations of these having generally been near the sea-coasts, and in some cases extending over quite large areas on both sides of the island; the numerous limestone caves have provided many skulls and relics of Indian origin. A series of rock-carvings with deep incisions representing human figures and heads, also rude outlines of lizards, birds, and turtles, have been found in the parish of St Catherine, possessing analogous features to similar finds in various West Indian islands. Implements too, such as chisels, axes, celts, mealing-stones, flaked flints, chalcedony beads, perforated ornamental shells, have been unearthed in different localities. Columbus spoke of the idols worshipped by the Indians of Jamaica, and it is interesting to learn that two stone images, probably examples of their gods, were sent home for exhibition by the Hon. D. Campbell; others, perforated behind for suspension, were found in a shell-heap, and probably were worn as amulets. In speaking of the Indians as the aborigines, it must be understood that this was a generic name applied indiscriminately to all the inhabitants of the lands discovered by Columbus, but the

Arawak tribe is distinct from the man-eating Caribs who lived near the regions of the Orinoco. In Mr im-Thurn's work, "Among the Indians of Guiana," he compares these prehistoric Jamaican objects with those of other West Indian islands, and the mainland of America, and finds that there are more notes of resemblance between them and those of the Indians, both ancient and modern, of British Guiana. With this last-named race, the former inhabitants of Jamaica, as well as many of the aborigines of other islands, are supposed to be most closely related.

It was one of these limestone caverns, where Indian remains had been found, that I visited, for it was in such hiding-places the poor Arawaks took refuge from the tender mercies of their Spanish conquerors, who, at the most moderate computation, accounted for some 60,000 of them before the English occupation under Cromwell. The entrance was up a path leading from the main road, and was by no means conspicuous, but once inside, the cave was spacious and lofty; the stalactites hanging from the roof were of a very curious formation. Two of Mrs M——'s children accompanied me, and an overseer, with two attendant "boys," carried torches. It was very rough walking and fearfully hot, slippery and wet here and there. In one place, which the children called the banqueting-hall, from its vast proportions and high roof, we startled thousands of rat-bats, who had taken up their habitation in the deep recesses of the stalactites which hung over our heads. Two were knocked over, and I secured one; they have bat's wings attached to a mouse-like body. At last we came to a full stop, an unscaleable barrier of rock barred our way; the other side, they told me, was one of those underground rivers so common in the Cockpit Country, of which I shall speak further on; they run through the interstices between the limestone rocks. However, we contented ourselves with what we had seen, and were glad enough to breathe fresh air after nearly an hour's subterranean exploration.

The West Indian way of living, especially on these pens, strikes one as being the most suitable to the climate. We rose before 7 A.M., coffee was ready on the verandah at 7.30. The mistress of the house fed her poultry, and looked after household matters till 11. I made my excursion to the cave, walked or sketched until that hour, when the household retired to their bedrooms, where baths had been prepared; we then made our toilet for the day. Breakfast, which was similar to our luncheon, was served at mid-day; tea about 3.30, before we went for a drive; dinner, being a moveable feast, according to whatever constituted the afternoon programme, was at any hour between 5 and 7. On this particular day the buggy had been lent for a funeral. The difficulties of providing for sudden emergencies of this nature in a hot country, in a hilly and sparsely-inhabited region, struck me forcibly. The seats and cover were removed from the carriage, upon which wooden planks were laid so as to make a kind of platform; on this the coffin rested. "There are some gruesome things connected with funerals in these parts, where a coffin, or 'box' has to be put together in a few hours," Mr M—— said. Often, when death seemed a certainty, they had to send out "boys" to collect the necessary deals for the coffin, and set about making it before the breath was out of a man's body. Unless the gravediggers were well primed with rum, said he, they would not dig the grave, "for fear of duppy springing up, buckra." But the corpse expectant may recover occasionally, and the coffin then is calmly kept for use at a future date. Having seen some graves on the estate, neatly bricked over and cemented, in one of my walks, I asked if they belonged to the family who had formerly lived at N——, when Mrs M—— explained to me that it was the custom, if a bereaved widower thought fit to take a second wife into his hut, to make a brick erection, firmly cemented together, over that part of his compound where the former partner of his life had been laid to rest, or at any rate over the spot where he thought he had buried her, for fear of being disturbed by her ghostly wanderings. She had once enquired of a negro, who was hard at work on his wife's grave, why he was taking so much trouble with it; he told her it was to "keep down duppy, missus."

A beautiful drive one afternoon to the Maggoty Falls on the Black River was one of the most exquisite I had in Jamaica. The falls were 13 miles away; part of the road lay over a savannah, where deadly poison lurked in morass and swamp, and no white man dared live too near to these breeding-places of the malarial mosquito. The exquisite peacock-green hues of the Black River water must be seen to be appreciated. On either bank profuse parasitical growth obscured the most majestic trees; tropical foliage was to be seen here at its very best.

The heat was most oppressive; it rained as we returned. The suffocating atmosphere in the lowlands made us glad to climb the steep hills which lay between us and my friend's estate.

The Black River is the only navigable one in the island; lighters bring their cargoes up a considerable distance into the interior of it. In this neighbourhood I remarked again the size of the cotton-tree, with the wonderful spurs it sends out from its roots. This is not the red silk cotton-tree of India and of Java, known as the Simal tree from the seed-vessel containing red silk cotton; the cotton-tree of Jamaica has seed-vessels containing white silk cotton. The Arawaks attached a religious importance to this tree, and at the present day the son of Ham regards it as the haunt and home of "duppies." The aboriginal idea was that "after the earth was made the Supreme Being, our Father, our Maker," made His throne in the cotton-tree. The legend of this Arawak belief is worthy of note, and I quote it as given by Bret:

> "Still no life was in the land,
> No sweet birds sang songs of love,
> O'er the plain and through the grove,
> Nothing then was seen to move.
> From that bright green throne His hand
> Scattered twigs and bark around,
> Some in air and some on land,
> Some the sparkling waters found.
> Soon He saw with life abound
> Water, air, and solid ground;
> Those which fell upon the stream
> Found a pleasant shelter there.
> Shining fishes dart and gleam
> Where those woody fragments were;
> Others sported through the air
> Bright with wings and feathers fair."

CHAPTER XIV
OBEAHISM AND COFFEE-PLANTING

It was whilst staying at this pen that I learnt a good deal on the subject of native negro superstitions.

I had been told by a coffee-planter, whose dealings with his black labourers had been somewhat acrimonious, that they had "set Obi" for him. Although the matter in dispute between him as landlord, and the negroes as tenants, amounted only to a few pounds, the latter, collectively, had paid as much as £25 to an Obeah man to Obi him. He had laughed at them, and had pointed out to them the futility of their spells and curses, so far as he and his health and prosperity were concerned.

"You can't Obi me. There's not a man among you good enough to Obi me," he told them. The black woolly pates had gone off to talk the matter over amongst themselves, and they had come to the same conclusion: they couldn't Obi a white man. So ingrained in them is this belief in the spell of their wizards, that I am told in the country parts, where their ignorance is still almost undiluted, that they look upon the "passon" as the white Obeah man.

I have not seen a negro grow pale at the mention of Obeah, but I have seen him squirm, and noted the expression of unqualified tenor spreading over his features as I enlarged upon the folly of it.

Mrs M——'s governess, who came from a parish some 20 miles down the Black River, told me that she knew by sight several of these champion swindlers, called "Obeah men," and that Obi prevailed largely in that neighbourhood notwithstanding the laws passed for its suppression.

Before proceeding further, I will quote from two authorities upon this subject of Obeahism which the professors of it originally brought from Africa. In fact there have been few estates which have not had their particular "Obeah man" in times past.

Mr Long says in his History of Jamaica, written about 1770: "The term Obeah, Obiah, or Obia we conceive to be the adjective and Obe or Obi the noun substantive, and that by the words Obia men or women are meant those who practise Obi."

Mr Bryan Edwards, writing at the beginning of last century and commenting upon the probable etymology of the word, says: "A serpent in the Egyptian language was called Ob or Aub. Obion is still the Egyptian name for a serpent. Moses, in the name of God, forbids the Israelites ever to inquire of the demon Ob, which is translated in our Bible charmer or wizard—*divinator aut sorcelegus*. The woman at Endor is called Oub, or Ob translated Pythonissa. Oubaris was the name of the Basilisk, or Royal serpent, emblem of the sun, and an ancient oracular deity of Africa. This derivation, which applies to one particular sect, the remnant probably of a very celebrated religious order in remote ages, is now become in Jamaica the general term to denote those Africans who in that island practise witchcraft or sorcery."

The Obeah man, as I have heard him described, is generally a most forbidding-looking person, craftiness and cunning being stamped on his features. He pretends to a medicinal knowledge of herbs, and undoubtedly is well versed in the action of subtle poisons; his trade is to impose upon his simple compatriot. The negro consults him in cases of illness, as well as to call down revenge upon his enemies for injuries sustained. It is wonderful how secret they keep their "Obeahism" from the white man. They always "set Obi" at midnight. In the morning the stoutest-hearted negro gives himself up for lost when he sees the well-known, but much dreaded insignia of the Obeah man upon his door-step, or under the thatch of the roof. This generally consists of a bottle with turkeys' or cocks' feathers stuck into it, with an accompaniment of parrots' beaks, drops of blood, coffin nails, and empty egg-shells. The same spirit of fatalism which makes the black tell you he cannot "dead" before his time, causes him to believe himself the victim of an unseen irresistible power. The dread of supernatural evil, which he is powerless to combat, acts upon what nervous system he possesses, so that sleep becomes an impossibility, his appetite fails him, his light-heartedness disappears as the ever-growing fear possesses his imagination more and more, and he generally dies. Whole plantations of slaves have been known to be almost depopulated by this extraordinary superstition. At one time the Obeah rites were so cruel, that the impostors, if caught, were hanged; flogging is now the punishment awarded to them. Naturally, the deaths by poison are ascribed to the powerful supernatural agency at work. If some black wiser than his fellows should suspect that other than Obeah influence was answerable for the death of his friend, his terrible dread of the awful vengeance which these wizards would work upon him would effectually restrain his tongue from betraying them. If a black man loses a pig or a sheep, he immediately has resource to the Obeah man, whom he pays as much as the latter can extort from him to "set Obi" for the thief. When the last-named rascal discovers this, he seeks out a more famous Obeah man to counteract the magic of the first. Should he find no one to undertake the job, he will probably fall into a decline from sheer fright of unknown calamity hanging over his head. Such is the story of their ignorant priestcraft. The law of Jamaica recognises "blood, feathers, parrots' beaks, dogs' teeth, alligators' teeth, broken bottles, grave-dirt, rum and egg-shells" as the unlawful stock-in-trade of the Obeah man. One of these gentlemen was hung in all the feathers and perquisites of his profession in 1760. He had come with other slaves from the Gold Coast and headed a revolt in a plantation in St Mary's Parish, but the panic-stricken negroes soon quieted down upon the death of their leader. This led to a discovery of their superstitious practices, which were immediately legislated against.

Bryan Edwards tells a story of a sugar-planter who, returning to Jamaica after a temporary absence in 1775, found that great mortality had taken place amongst his slaves, the remaining number of them being in a lamentable condition. He tried his hardest to find out the cause of the depopulation of his estate, but without success. At length he had reason to suspect Obi. A negress, who had long been ill, one day confessed to him that the reason of her sickness was that her old stepmother of eighty had "put Obi" upon her, and that she had done the same to those who had died off so quickly. The other slaves on the property admitted that since she had come from Africa she had carried on this trade and was the terror of the place. The owner of the plantation immediately searched the hut of this hoary-headed witch, with the result that inside the thatched roof the whole of the miserable materia Obeah was found. In addition to the usual feathers and rags an earthen pot was found under the bed containing quantities of round clay balls variously compounded, some with hair, or rags, or stuck round with dogs' or cats' teeth, also egg-shells filled with a gummy substance which, unfortunately, was not subjected to a rigid analysis. The hut was burnt; the old woman was not hung, but sold to some Spaniards who took her to Cuba. History does not record her performances further. But once removed from the scene of her evil practices, the slaves lost their fear, and the mortality amongst them ceased. The proprietor estimated he had lost a hundred negroes in fifteen years from the practice of Obeahism.

There is no doubt that superstition, which always goes hand-in-hand with ignorance, is born and bred in the descendants of Ham. Nowhere, I learn, is this more the case than amongst the Jamaican negroes inhabiting the mountainous parts of the island. In the Blue Mountains, where wooded heights and musical murmuring streams suggest supernatural agencies, one finds weird ideas among their folk-lore. If you can persuade some native to talk about the "duppy," you may learn that that which is most feared is a rolling calf; you will be told how the sight of it foretells great misfortune, and those who have witnessed the awful phantom describe it as a huge animal with fire issuing from its nostrils, and clanking chains as it rolls down the mountain-side, burning everything in its path. Other apparitions of a cat as large as a goat, with eyes burning like vast lamps, are said to have been seen by the mountain dwellers at nightfall in the woods. Some of these story-tellers will eat a raw rat before relating the ghost stories, to give them, as they express it, a "sweet mout."

Indeed, it was during our conversation on the verandah one morning when one of their strange notions was forcibly brought to my notice. The three boys of the family, after their early coffee at 7.30, had gone for a ride, and a swim in the river; on their return an altercation was heard in the dining-room, and the eldest son came and showed his mother where Theodora, one of the black maids, had actually bitten him. The children had scuffled, the servant lost her temper, and actually bit the boy till the blood came, and then cursed him. Needless to say, she was very soon packed off. But Mrs M—— explained to me that to curse with blood in the mouth is quite a usual practice with them. Any amount of Obi, said she, is secretly practised in country parts and in secluded mountain parishes in spite of the most carefully-framed laws against it. Since the police officials are mostly black, one can easily understand how the culprits may be shielded. The same thing holds good with petty theft, of which everybody having property in Jamaica whom I met complained bitterly. On this pen where I stayed, fowls were frequently taken, yams also and bananas; two years before they had lost a cow and calf. The thieves were never discoverable, though the local police called at the house occasionally, to get their books signed, to show they had faithfully executed their rounds.

To return to our subject, I read in an American magazine that one of the well-known Obeah poisons is made as follows. The negro takes the juice of the cassava plant, which he squeezes on to a copper pan, and places it in the sun. The most horrible insects are the result, which are dried and ground to a powder. The Obeah man or woman drops into the victim's coffee or soup a tiny particle of this powder, which produces death without leaving a trace of the drug. Some of their poisons induce insanity.

I heard of a black servant-girl who tried to murder her mistress by putting ground glass in her soup. It was fortunately discovered in time, but not before the young woman had absconded, leaving no trace behind her.

Some planters adopt Obi to ensure themselves against thieving. They take a large black bottle, fill it with some phosphorescent liquid, and place within it the feather of a buzzard, the quill sticking uppermost. This they fasten to a tree on the outskirts of their coffee-patch or banana-field, where it can be well observed by all who pass near. The dusky population, firmly believing it to be the work of the Obeah man, refrain their thieving propensities accordingly. I was told, too, how their fatalism causes them to cruelly neglect their sick.

Not long since an aged labourer on a neighbouring plantation was attacked with disease. The proprietor ordered special food to be cooked for him, and a servant was told off to look after him. The latter never went near the old black, so the result was that the master, who was a good-hearted man, took personal charge of him, whilst his wife brought food to him, even cooking it herself. The old negro, however, died, and then the friends, who had not been near him for days, crowded to the little hut, and not only had the corpse laid out in a fine new suit of white duck, but held a wake for three nights, when they disposed of enough rum and tea, in celebrating his decease, to have kept the old fellow going months during his lifetime.

A very usual complaint amongst the black women in Jamaica is the information that they have a pain. "Missus, I'se got a pain!" has been said to me in my walks in the country, the tone of voice being sepulchrally solemn.

They have a patent treatment for fever, called the "bush bath." This consists of equal proportions of the leaves of the following plants: akee, sour sop, jointwood, pimento, cowfoot, elder, lime-leaf and liquorice. The patient is plunged into the bath when it is very hot, and is covered with a sheet. When the steam has penetrated the skin, the patient is removed from the bath, and covered with warm blankets, leaving the skin undried. A refreshing sleep is invariably the consequence, and a very perceptible fall in temperature.

There is a native disease called "yaws," which the natives treat in their own fashion. The patient's feet are held in boiling water, this, however, is not so successful a treatment as the former, for I was told it generally results in sending the chill inward, and often pneumonia is the result.

I had mentioned to my kind host and hostess that a visit to their coffee-works would be of great interest to me, so one day I was shown over the building by the overseer. I have since been on other plantations, and I find the proprietors of these estates all agree in saying that unless a man has capital, it is no good coming out to Jamaica for a living, and then he should live at least one or two years on a coffee estate before he purchases land and sets up for himself. The authorities at Hope Gardens, the Government botanical gardens at Kingston, told me it was precisely the same thing with bananas. Many men have lost money through not knowing the soils suitable for planting coffee. In starting a plantation, or patch—which latter means a clearing on a hill, or, in the case of bananas, a bit of fertile valley near a stream—the young trees are usually planted 8 feet apart; some even prefer to give them more distance. At the end of the third year a small crop is generally gathered, sufficient to pay expense of cultivation. The fourth year should yield a good crop; the trees, according to the soil, will bear from thirty to forty years. The coffee berries when ripe are bright purple-red, looking much like cherries. The coffee kernels, like cherry-stones, are encased in the flesh of the fruit.

The berries are, first of all, run through a "pulper"; this machine tears off the pulp from the kernel. The next part of the process is to run them into tanks filled with water, where they are occasionally shaken, to wash off any remaining pulp left on them. Then they are removed from the tanks and spread out in the sun on great platforms made of cement, and left exposed till quite dry. These platforms are called "patios" or "barbecues"; the former is the Spanish for courtyard, the latter word was used by the aborigines to designate the smooth places on which they dried their fish and fruit. At one side of each barbecue a shed is always constructed into which the coffee is swept in case of rain. The coffee, when thoroughly dried, is removed from the patio. As far as this point the two kernels which form the stone, so to speak, of the berry, and which lie with their flat surfaces face to face, are surrounded by a horny covering, sometimes called the parchment skin, or silver skin. To remove this the coffee is run through a mill properly constructed for the purpose. It is then ready to be shipped, but in the coffee mill I visited, the coffee was sorted according to size. This "grading the kernels" was done by a very simple machine similar to one used by wholesale dealers in England. Coffee used to fetch 80s. and 90s. for 100 lbs.—now the planter rarely gets more than 25s. for the same quantity. Estates in the Blue Mountains, which at one time yielded a return to their owner of £5000 a year, at present scarcely bring in as many hundreds. The labour question has, of course, something to do with the difference in returns. In times of slavery an estate such as I have mentioned was worked by perhaps two hundred slaves. At the present day the black will not go so far in the mountains if he can get labour nearer home, and to expect him to work more than three days a week is to expect that the heavens will rain gold for the asking. The hillside coffee-pickers are said to be the least intelligent of the negroes; they live far from towns, where their brethren absorb a smattering of education without effort. These coffee-pickers, who speak an almost unintelligible jargon of their own, in which Spanish words, African, and even Indian expressions are often intermingled, are paid by the bushel and earn more than in the sugar-fields; the majority get as much as 2s. a day. On arriving from the plantations the hands pour their gathering into the measures of the overseers, whence it goes straight to the pulping machines.

It is very clean work, and the women who set the fashion to their fellows repair to coffee-picking and sorting in their best clothes. A favourite drink with them is called matrimony, and is made of equal parts of the pulp and juice of the orange and the star-apple mixed with sugar and a dash of rum. Another confection to which the black palate is partial is a paste made of brown sugar and grated cocoa-nut. In a list supplied by the Merchants' Exchange, I read that 69,128 cwt. of coffee was exported from Jamaica between April 1902 and January 1903, against 49,811 cwt. between April 1901 and January 1902, which shows the industry is prospering. The Colonial Secretary, Mr Ollivier, attributes the low prices prevailing to the enormous crops produced in the Brazils of late. Referring to the lack of water for the proper washing of coffee, which is the case in some parts of the island, where the natives are even too lazy to build tanks for their domestic supply, he urges combination for central plant, and says: "Despite the low prices, if in those districts where the coffee is not pulped and washed the settlers who grow the bulk of our ordinary coffee were to combine, as they have done in some instances, to obtain pulping machines and hulling mills and to cure their coffee properly, there can be no doubt that the export value of our coffee would be increased by about 25 per cent. During the fluctuations of the last two years the prices of these better cured coffees have kept comparatively steady, although at lower prices than formerly." In a local newspaper of the 2nd of March the leading article is devoted to the increased prosperity and more promising outlook for the coming year. It is quite refreshing to think there may be a good time in store for this pearl of the Caribbean Sea, after the dismal prophecies and pessimistic whinings of the inert and apathetic who abound in Jamaica.

A cablegram, according to this organ of the press, had just been received from the *Daily Mail*, giving the information that a group of English, Italian, and Brazilian capitalists are forming a trust to monopolise the coffee trade of Brazil. It says that the syndicate is being supported by the Brazilian government, and goes on to state that "it is expected that prices will be raised 30 per cent." This is a piece of welcome news and of most noteworthy importance to all the growers of coffee from one end of Jamaica to the other, since the price of that article, with the exception of the coffee grown amongst the Blue Mountains, is fixed by the price that is paid for Brazilian coffee. And if such a remarkable rise in that article should take place, "as is foreshadowed in the cable despatch," it will result in a period of prosperity for the planters of Jamaica such as possibly they have dreamt of, but never expected to experience.

CHAPTER XV
COCKPIT COUNTRY—THE MAROONS

If there is one thing more interesting to the unbiassed traveller than others, it is to hear and analyse the various opinions expressed upon the subject he or she is attempting to master in the spirit of disinterestedness and liberal judgment, by those whose lives are being lived in that particular spot of the globe temporarily under review.

"England has treated Jamaica abominably," I frequently heard. She had insisted on the liberation of the slaves, then inadequately compensated their owners, and when their emancipation upset all prevailing conditions of labour, instead of protecting sugar, the chief industry of her West Indian colonies, and fostering its growth, she fairly knocked it on the head by the introduction of free trade. When beetroot-sugar first arrived in Jamaica the nails were driven into its coffin. Annexation to the United States was not desirable, it was declared, but, so far as business was concerned, America would make things hum.

The negroes were emancipated too soon, thought certain of the grumblers. Had the Jamaican blacks been as well educated as their brothers in the States at the time they became freed, they would have a different race of peasants in the island to-day. "They will never make citizens," I was told. They have no idea of the responsibilities of a civilised community; even those who had voting powers on local questions were too lazy or too callous to record their votes. If a white man suggested to them how better to cultivate their patch of land, or if the coffee-curers and shippers, for instance, advised them to bring their coffee when picked straight to their mills where they had the proper apparatus for curing the beans, the blacks would immediately suspect the white man had "something up his sleeve," and was going to get the better of them in some underhand way.

Things, no doubt, are difficult in Jamaica under the very best of circumstances. The negro is unquestionably a low type of humanity, naturally unintelligent and lazy. People forget, however, he has, in the first place, only recently discovered that he has a soul as well as the white man, and, in the second place, but just learnt, the other day as it were, to call that soul his own.

Nearly two centuries of abject slavery, with its accompaniments of forced labour and hard usage, have passed over his head, since, as a free savage, he roamed the African forests, a fetich-worshipper, the victim of the lowest superstitions, and practising every vice known to humanity. Evangelising efforts were spasmodically made here and there to ameliorate the condition of the plantation slaves by those whose conscience was in advance of their times; but when in 1834 the yoke of slavery was removed with such an ancestry, such a history behind them, what could a reasonable person expect of the sons and daughters of Ham! The planters had regarded them as the necessary machinery for producing their princely incomes when the wealth of the West Indian merchant was a known quantity. To improve the breed the physically-fittest were, like cattle, carefully selected, and the women told off for this purpose given especially lighter work to perform. This practice alone might account for much of the indiscriminate living which called forth the blazing indignation and burning words of one of the Keswick delegates, whose work is mentioned on a former page.

The injustice of his wholesale indictment against the character of the women of this island is still felt by many.

One clergyman, of over thirty years' experience in Jamaica, and whose church numbers 1300 communicants, expressed to me his strong disapproval of the way in which this island was held up as a "plague spot" for its wickedness, by persons who had no practical knowledge either of its history or its inhabitants.

If in the year 1902, 62 per cent. of the children born are illegitimate, in 1834, had a census been taken, probably there would have been over 90 per cent. Of the present 62 per cent., given by the latest returns, I was assured that fifty out of that number would represent the children of persons living together in faithful, though unwedded union.

It is a matter of history that white overseers on the estates were dismissed on their marriage for obvious reasons. Every obstacle was placed upon the marriage of slaves; I believe on many estates it was forbidden. Then the example set by the whites has been most shameful throughout the history of Jamaica in this respect. Considering these circumstances, and the very recent growth of any sort of moral standard, one is not surprised to hear many persons speak indignantly of the Keswick delegates and the superficial nature of their work.

It is not inconceivable that the forefathers of these gentlemen, who were so incredibly shocked at the immorality of Jamaica, might have been planters themselves in distant times; and if their lot were cast in such homes as house the peasantry of Jamaica they might not escape that fall which seems the common lot of unregenerated humanity. Let the ardent reformers who advertised the island as a "plague spot," and who would dragoon this childish race into a code of morality, remember that a great deal is attributable to the cupidity of the white man who violated the principles of humanity to procure the "foul tissue of terrestrial gold."

The very handsome marble monuments sent out from England, erected to the memory of many of these, adorn the walls of the island churches, and speak from their sacred precincts to the silent observer. Here other than the poetic-minded may gather as he wanders

> "Wisdom from the central deep,
> And, listening to the inner flow of things,
> Speak to the age out of eternity."

Now, it appears to my limited range of vision that from brute animalism both Church and State, working into each other's hands, are making the race into useful men and women. They know now something of the sacredness of marriage and family life, as well as of the arts of civilisation. In an interesting article entitled "Among the Jamaican Negroes," by an American lady, Mrs K. J. Hall, published in the October issue 1902 of a magazine known as *The World To-day*, the situation is admirably summed up in these words: "Deceitfulness and untruthfulness are the besetting sins of the race, though the educated are bravely struggling with their less enlightened kinsmen. Each year witnesses some forward step taken by these people so lately freed from bondage."

It was with regret that I took leave of my kind friends at N——, and prepared to extend my journey to the extreme limit of the railway, which ends at Montego Bay, a port on the northern coast. I had first, however, to traverse that part of the island known as the Cockpit Country, parts of which being remarkably beautiful. From an agricultural standpoint, this mountainous stretch is practically useless. Isolated peaks covered with tropical foliage form a background to a vast labyrinth of glades and valleys separating precipitous cliffs. Here and there a few smoother tracts occur, and at other places a whole series of impassable sink-holes, called cockpits, prevent further progress. At the bottom of these deep valleys the inhabitants grow a banana-patch, and very sparsely over this hilly country-side does one catch glimpses of the wattled huts of the blacks. I believe the country has never yet been thoroughly explored; it offers first-rate facilities for a traveller to lose himself in. At the present day it is the home of the Maroons, but these latter have no distinguishing facial characteristics by which to recognise them, the negro type being everywhere predominant. There is very little water in these parts, for the rain is carried off directly by numerous crevices. Springs, long distances apart, form underground water-courses, and, coming to the surface, disappear again. These are sink-holes; they are generally to be found deep down in some valley. The character of the ground around them plainly indicates their existence; but occasionally such openings are to be met with on more level ground, where nothing whatever gives a sign of danger, grass and brush growing over the edge of the aperture and concealing it from observation, until the unwary victim steps unconsciously over the brink of the treacherous chasm, and disappears, to be seen no more. Persons have been known to drop out of life thus into a deep unfathomable grave.

In the south-western part of St Ann's Parish, which for its exquisite beauty has been called the "Garden of Jamaica," there is an opening into the subterranean passages amongst the mountains, associated with the most shocking tragedies attended by circumstances of unusual horror. This sink-hole is called "Hutchinson's Hole." Near by is the ruined home of the monster, who was at length brought to justice for a whole catalogue of atrocities; it is still known by the name of "Hutchinson's Tower." Travellers who sought hospitality at this house, which was miles away from any other habitation, obtained it, but they invariably met with the cruel fate which their host had in reserve for all who approached his domain, their bodies afterwards being thrown down "Hutchinson's Hole." At length, being discovered, he fled; the whole country rose up in pursuit. At Old Harbour Hutchinson found a boat, and put off to sea. Lord Rodney was then in command of the fleet at Port Royal; hearing of the miscreant's flight from justice, he set sail in his own ship, and speedily overhauled the merchantman which had taken the fugitive on board, captured him, and he was afterwards hung at Spanish Town.

The geological explanation is that the foundation of the limestone hills is probably coral reef, the rough country lying between these reefs a formation caused by the sedimentary deposit produced by the action of the sea. After the volcanic upheaval of Jamaica it is thought that these limestone basins gradually found drainage under the surrounding mountains, and this, through successive ages of disintegration, has brought these districts to their present rough almost impassable structure. The railway affords most beautiful views as it curves round the mountains after having skirted, for some miles, the Black River on the level country. After crossing the third bridge, it commences to ascend into this wild and picturesque region. Some of the gradients are very steep, and the curves very sharp; but the views to be obtained from apparently perilous heights into the deep valleys below are well worth the journey.

> Miss Sarah Elsey Cole
> Bo.t of William Ramsay
> 1804
> July 24. One New Negro Girl from the
> Windward Coast — £90. —
> Received payment
> Will.m Ramsay.

I have mentioned that this is the home of the Maroons, and I cannot do better at this part of my travels than sketch the events which led to their segregation in these mountains. This involves a dip into the origin of modern slavery. Since the fall of the Roman Empire, and the rise of Christendom, slavery was almost unknown in Europe excepting in the serfdom of Moscovy until, in 1442, the Portuguese explorer, Prince Henry, whilst sailing down the African coast, compelled Antony Gonsalez, his countryman, to restore some Moors to their home whom he had seized as prisoners, some two years previously, in the neighbourhood of Cape Bojador. The wily Gonsalez obeyed the prince, but received in exchange ten blacks and some gold dust, which he took back to Lisbon. His friends and acquaintances evidently thought to do a roaring trade in following his footsteps, so they fitted out thirty ships to pursue this traffic.

In 1481 the Portuguese built three forts, one on the Gold Coast, one on an adjacent island, the other at Loango—their king assuming the title of Lord of Guinea! From this date the western continent, so recently discovered, was furnished with slaves. In 1502 the Spaniards employed them to work in the mines of Hispaniola, but we read that the governor forbade the traffic, as the negroes taught the Indians knowledge of their evil ways. But the latter becoming scarcer, owing to the cruelty of their conquerors, the Emperor, Charles V., granted a patent to certain persons giving them the monopoly of supplying four thousand negroes annually to Hispaniola, Cuba, Jamaica, and Porto Rico. Herrera, the Spanish historian of those days, tells us that this patent was assigned to Genoese merchants. From that time the slave trade was an established and regular business.

Nor have we, nationally speaking, clean hands in this respect. Sir John Hawkins Knight, commander of Queen Elizabeth's navy, found, says Hakluyt, "that negroes were very good merchandise, and that stores of negroes might easily be had on the coast of Guiney"; he resolved to make trial thereof, and communicated that device with his worshipful friends of London. He sailed to Sierra Leone in 1562. Two hundred years later, so great a trade had this become, that a list was prepared by the Liverpool merchants for the Privy Council 1772. In it we find in one year 74,000 slaves were exported. The British headed the list with 38,000, the French followed with 20,000, the Dutch 4000, Danes 2000, and the Portuguese 10,000. They were captured from Gambia, Sierra Leone, Cape Palmas, Gold Coast, Whydah, Lagos, and Benin, Bonny, and New Calabar, the Cameroons, Loango and Benguela principally.

It was Homer who said: "The day which makes a man a slave takes away half his worth," and in the nature of things it must be so.

Surely our complicity and share in these dark days is being atoned for in the efforts to benefit the black race. The stings of the national conscience have been severe, but the growth in grace of our legislators a certainty.

Cheap cotton fabrics, specially manufactured to clothe their dusky limbs, come from Manchester. Food of the best and of the cheapest is within their reach; and I was even told by a landowner not long since, that it was no good going to law for the petty thieving which is so irritating, because "the judges favoured the blacks"!

The Maroons, who inhabit the Cockpit Country as well as a town called Moore Town, near Port Antonio, on the north coast, are still known by that name, although there is practically nothing in their appearance to differentiate them from the rest of the black and coloured races. The word is derived from the Spanish *marrano*, signifying, "a young pig." The hardy-looking mountaineers one sees from the carriage window of the train, clad in the very sketchiest of clothing, are the descendants of fierce and warlike slaves of mixed African and Indian blood who, on the conquest of Jamaica by the Cromwellian troops, escaped to the hills, and defied the new possessors of the island to conquer them.

There seems every reason to believe that when Columbus first discovered Jamaica it was thickly populated by the Arawaks.

Bartholomew de las Casas, Bishop of Chiapa, compares the aboriginal Indians to "ants on an ant-hill"; probably this referred to the inhabitants of the lowlands and savannahs on the coasts.

This Spanish prelate, who figured in history as the protector and advocate of the Indians, gave, however, his episcopal consent to the patent issued by Charles V., granting to the merchants of Genoa the monopoly of the slave trade with the Indies. A writer, noting the inconsistency of character in the man who, in order to preserve and protect one of the most interesting aboriginal races of the world, concurred in the subjugation and slavery of another, says of him: "While he contended for the liberty of the people born in one quarter of the globe, he laboured to enslave the inhabitants of another region, and in the warmth of his zeal to save the Americans from the yoke, pronounced it to be lawful and expedient to impose one still heavier upon the Africans." Such are the extraordinary contradictions the page of history reveals to us. It is equally curious to read of a plantation with its complement of slaves in Barbadoes having been left to The Society in Great Britain for the Propagation of the Gospel, by a certain Colonel Codrington, which, says Bryan Edwards, "had to continue the disagreeable necessity of supporting slavery bequeathed to than, still more to occasionally purchase more slaves to keep up the stock." It would scarcely be profitable or edifying, possibly, in these days, to search too closely as to how certain moneys left to charitable institutions were first obtained, but the idea of funds devoted to the lofty and elevating purposes of extending a knowledge of the Bible amongst the heathen coming from West Indian slave plantations, appears to me of unique interest.

The way in which the Spaniards treated the harmless and inoffensive Indians is well known, and has never been better described than by Charles Kingsley in "Westward Ho!" To the rough-and-ready sailor of the days of Queen Bess, to fight the Spaniard and to fight the devil were one and the same thing. Nor, so far as their character for cruelty goes, is the modern Spaniard one whit better than his ancestors. The writer of these pages spent a few weeks travelling in Spain, in the spring of 1902, and was impressed by the national bloodthirstiness, as exhibited in the great ardour and passionate enthusiasm displayed over everything connected with the peninsular pastime of bull-fighting. The callousness to suffering, and the innate love of cruelty, shown by the labouring classes and by the aristocracy of Spain, as when looking round the crowded amphitheatre to escape from the disgusting sights and sounds of the arena, one noted the expression of absorbed interest over every gory detail of the fight, were painfully apparent. Old women pawn their beds, and girls sell their tresses of hair, to be able, at least once a year, to attend a bull-fight. The Pope has expressed his abhorrence of it, whilst, it is well known, Queen Christina equally detests it; but such is the force of the national love of the sport, that any dynasty endeavouring to suppress it might count its days as numbered. It is no matter of surprise to read amongst the island chronicles that in Jamaica and the adjacent islands the Spaniards destroyed, within less than twenty years, more than 1,200,000 of the native Indians, when one rightly appreciates the devilry of the Spaniard. It was on account of the disappearance of these aborigines that African labour was first brought across the Atlantic, and owing to the gradual extermination of the Indians in Hispaniola, and in the Spanish-American possessions generally, slavery became a systematised traffic. Naturally these persons, who had so inhumanly treated the poor Arawaks—and they seem to have been a mild and gentle type of savage, very different from the Caribs, who were cannibals, and who confined their attentions to the eastern islands of the Caribbean Sea—could not be expected to treat the African with greater consideration. When one thinks of the blood-curdling stories of the atrocities committed by the subjects of the Spanish Crown, both on Indians and Africans alike, and then of the ferocity and native savagery of the negro in his reprisals—for when the blacks got the upper hand their uprisings against and massacres of their white masters are amongst the most horrible in the history of the world—one shudders at the thought of what, if they could speak, the mountain fastnesses, the waving cane-fields, could tell!

One of the punishments which existed among the Spaniards was, that a slave failing to fulfil the task assigned to him, was liable to be buried up to his neck, and to be left to be devoured by insects!

Historians have unanimously declared the Arawaks to have been a simple, quiet folk, neither ferocious nor treacherous, their government patriarchal and dignified. They smoked tobacco from a quaint sort of pipe, consisting of a straight tube branching off into two others, which they inserted up their nostrils. Why, indeed, so kindly and so superior a race should, in the foreknowledge of Providence, have been permitted to be superseded in this island by the unintelligent and degraded black of tropical Africa is an inscrutable problem to human ken. The Arawak was an enlightened savage. He mixed very little superstition with his theology. He believed in the existence of a Supreme Being, all-powerful and invisible, whom he worshipped under the name of Iocahuna; besides, he venerated a lower order of household and other gods. One reads that these people had peculiar ideas of the creation of the world, and I have already alluded to the veneration in which they held the cotton-tree as the throne of the Creator, also that they, in common with many aboriginal races, had traditions about a deluge. They believed in a future state of existence which, if it differed from the happy hunting-ground of the North-American Indian's paradise, was to be a place of perfect happiness. To the limited faculties of the Arawak, that would be represented by sensual enjoyments more than anything else.

An anecdote, giving an idea of the estimation in which the Spaniards were held by the native Indians, is related by the Rev. J. B. Ellis: "A cacique or chief fled to Cuba, to escape his European tormentors, having in his possession a valuable casket of gold. When pursued by the Spaniards, he conceived the idea of propitiating the Spanish Deity. 'Behold,' he said, pointing to the golden box, 'the God of the Europeans'; and summoning his friends and attendants, he held a mighty feast in honour of this deity, offering sacrifices, and singing and dancing around the precious box. Still the Spaniards approached in their pursuit; and Hatuey, the cacique, told his companions that they must be rid entirely of the God of the Spaniards before they could hope to be free from their persecuting presence. Accordingly, the golden casket was solemnly buried in the sea. Nevertheless, Hatuey was captured, and promptly condemned to be burned alive. While the necessary preparations for his execution were being made, a friar attempted to convert and baptise the unhappy cacique, enlarging much on the happiness of a future heaven. 'In this heaven of yours,' asked the condemned man, 'are there any Spaniards?' 'Certainly,' answered the friar, 'but they are all good Spaniards.' 'The best of them are good for nothing,' retorted Hatuey, 'and I will not go where I am likely to meet one of that awful tribe.'"

Let us return to our Maroons, who retreated into the hills before the English conquerors of the island. In after years, runaway slaves and disaffected persons fled to them, thus making them, for over a century and a half, a formidable antagonist to the colonist in the lower-lying plains near the coast. From the mountain fastnesses they harassed the English soldiery. Those who carelessly rambled from camps, or from the protection of their companions, were mercilessly slaughtered with that refinement of cruelty, in most cases, which makes the annals of the history of this island written, as it were, in human blood. How they intimidated the peaceful dwellers by their incessant and bloody raids, their burnings, and their hideous slaughtering, it can do no good to describe. To be "marooned" was a fate too horrible to contemplate, even in those days when life was of not so much account as we estimate it to-day.

Their dialect was a barbarous mixture of African and Spanish. They practised polygamy; the women did what labour was requisite, and Obeah-worship was the only religion they knew. They had been a thorn in the side of the English military occupation for many years. At last, in 1734, Captain Stoddart attacked them in the Blue Mountains so skilfully and so successfully that for a time they could do no more mischief in those parts; but the snake was only "scotched," not exterminated. Again it raised its hydra-head, and in 1736, a formidable movement under a leader named Cudgoe had to be suppressed. After this there seems to have been a desultory guerilla warfare, the enemy never appearing in the open, but sneaking round the plantations; many whites were killed in this way. However, in 1738, Governor Trelawny made a treaty with them, assigning them certain lands to live in.

If I have depicted the mildness of character of the extinct Arawak, I will here mention what Bryan Edwards says of the West African black:—

"The distinguishing features of the Gold Coast negroes are firmness of mind and body, ferocious dispositions, but, withal, activity, courage, and stubbornness, which prompt them to enterprises of difficulty and danger, enabling them to meet death, in its most horrible shape, with fortitude or indifference." This, he goes on to relate, was shown in the rebellion of 1760. A negro, who had been a chief of his tribe in Guinea, was imported with a hundred of his countrymen into Jamaica, and sold together to the owner of a plantation, on the frontier of St Mary's Parish. At his instigation, although they had received no ill-treatment since their arrival, they revolted. Gathering themselves together in a body they proceeded at midnight to Port Maria, where they slaughtered the sentinel, and went off with all the arms and ammunition they could lay hands on. Here they were joined by many runaway slaves, and, retreating to the interior of the island, they killed everybody they met, leaving desolation in their track.

At a plantation called Bellard's Valley they surrounded the overseer's house at four in the morning, butchered every soul on the place with the utmost savagery, and actually drank the blood of their victims mixed with rum. Wherever they went the same ghastly tragedies took place. In one morning they murdered forty whites and mulattoes.

At length Tacky, the chief, was fortunately killed in the woods; some of the principal ringleaders were taken at the same time, but, as there was every appearance of a general insurrection breaking out in the various adjacent plantations, the authorities decided to make a few terrible examples of the most guilty.

However horrible the details are, one feels that no more blame can be attached to those who framed such sentences than to those officers in the Indian rebellion of 1858 who condemned Sepoys to be blown from the cannon. One of these Guinea slaves was condemned to be burnt, two others to be hung up in irons and left to perish. The former was compelled to sit upon the ground, his body being chained to an iron stake.

One wonders if he had such a thing as a nervous system at all, for he complacently looked on as the fire was first lighted at his feet, and without a groan saw his legs reduced to ashes, after which, says Bryan Edwards, "one of his arms getting loose he flung a brand from the fire into the face of the executioner." The two which were hung up alive were indulged, at their own request, with a hearty meal just before being suspended on a gibbet which was put up in the parade of Kingston. From the time they were first placed there until the time they died, not a word of complaint did they utter, excepting to remark upon the chilliness of the night. All day long they amused themselves in talking to their brother Africans, who were permitted by the authorities, "very improperly to surround the gibbet. On the seventh day," says Edwards, whose description is that of an eye-witness, "a notion prevailed amongst the spectators that one of them wished to communicate an important secret to his master, my dear relative, who, being in St Mary's Parish, the commanding officer sent for me. I endeavoured by means of an interpreter to let him know I was present, but I could not understand what he said in return. I remember that both he and his fellow-sufferer laughed immoderately at something that occurred—I know not what. The next morning one of them silently expired, as did the other on the morning of the ninth day."

In the Museum which is attached to the Institute and Library of Kingston a gruesome relic is exhibited. It represents an iron cage, and was unearthed some years ago in the parish of St Andrews. It encloses the bones of a woman, and is constructed so as to fit the human body with bands around the neck, breast, and loins; there are bars to confine the legs, and stirrups for the feet, which have sharp pikes to press into the soles of the occupant's feet. There is a ring at the top of the structure to suspend it gibbet-wise. One can well understand the reluctance and the dread with which the sugar-planters regarded the passing of the Emancipation Bill.

To be overrun by a newly-liberated race of semi-savages was not an exhilarating thing to contemplate. Their standpoint was a very different one in all its bearings than that of the benevolent aristocrats in England, who discussed the measure at their ease, mutually congratulating themselves and the nation that at last they had obeyed the promptings of conscience.

CHAPTER XVI

INDIAN CATTLE AT MONTPELIER— PALMER MONUMENT IN MONTEGO BAY PARISH CHURCH—AMERICANS

After winding through the mountainous regions of the Cockpit Country, the train traverses a part known as Surinam Quarters. When the Dutch settled here in 1672 they intermarried with the negroes, and the whole of this section is peopled by their descendants. The next place of importance on the line is Montpelier, where there is a capital hotel. Here many people stay and drive the 10 miles, or so, down to Montego Bay. I had friends to meet at the last-named place, where I had heard of comfortable quarters, which, however, could not compare with the accommodation provided at Montpelier Hotel. In the vicinity there are two large estates owned by a wealthy Englishman, the Hon. Evelyn Ellis, who imported from India at great cost the famous Zebu and Mysore cattle; one can see in rambling over this neighbourhood their silver-gray hides and curious shapes. They were imported for labour and breeding purposes. The offspring of these Indian cattle when crossed with the native animal make the most useful stock for draft on sugar estates. These grazing pens are far-famed, and cover thousands of acres; enormous herds of cattle roam over them. I did not visit the tobacco fields and cigar factory here, though I believe they are most interesting. Neither did I take the coach, which runs between Montpelier and Savanna-la-Mar, 24 miles away on the south coast of the island, which is a most interesting and prosperous little seaport. Its one street, they say, is made from ships' ballast dumped down there by vessels loading with sugar. This road passes another famous pen, that of Knockalava, the property of Lord Malcolm, who has imported specimens of the celebrated Hereford breed of cattle at great expense. Besides these breeds the Ayrshire, Devon, Shorthorn, and East Indian are all represented in the island breeds.

The demand for cattle for working in the cane-fields has been the reason of grazing farms having reached their importance in the commercial and agricultural development of Jamaica, the result being that the selection of cows for milking purposes has been little considered. For those interested in farming I note that four-year-old steers, broken to the yoke, vary from £20 to £30 per pair, costing about £7 a head to raise. Hindu cattle fetch the highest prices, on account of their quickness and powers of endurance, added to which they stand the heat better than other breeds. I was told that sheep do not compare favourably with other live stock, although I never tasted better mutton than I did at Mandeville.

As the train emerges from a tunnel high above sea-level the most beautiful view is obtained of Montego Bay, which derives its name from *manteca*, the Spanish for "hog lard," and carries one back to the days of the occupation of the Spaniard when lard was shipped from this port in large quantities. During the two last centuries, the place was the centre of the sugar industry; since its failure it has resurrected itself again in the fruit trade.

No more lovely panoramic view of bay, islands, town, and green cane-fields could be found than the one I looked down upon, as descending a fairly steep but circuitous gradient, we approached the plain beneath. The little coral atolls, known as the Bogue Islands, are extremely interesting, and their shape and circular formation can nowhere better be seen than before the station is reached.

The little town presents nothing of any importance to describe. Like all West Indian urban resorts, the dust is ever with you. I drove to my destination, "Miss Harrison, on the Hill." A very loquacious driver whirled me through the long street, then round a sharp corner, another to the left, and then, lashing his emaciated-looking horses, he drove them up a steep ascent over stones, projecting rocks, anything and everything, at the top of which, on a sloping declivity, he skilfully turned the conveyance round so that I should step out at the entrance. I am not naturally nervous, having been used to horses in an old country home, and I suppose driven them since I was big enough to be trusted with reins; but Heaven is my witness that nothing but a philosophical mental review of the chances against my being the first one of "Miss Harrison on the Hill's" guests to come to grief kept me spell-bound on the back part of the shandry-dan belonging to her establishment. I went up a stone flight of steps leading to the living apartments of what seemed to me a very curiously Continental-looking house, built on the side of the hill, but from the windows of which, with their little quaint balconies in front, a magnificent view of the setting sun showed crimson and gold between palm-leaves and bougainvillia, the latter adorning the front of the house. Miss Harrison, an ancient coloured lady, introduced herself to me. She told me she owned the house, and that her father was Scotch; she also showed me, with some pride, her grandchildren. I did not press her to tell me any more of her family history, but, asking for some hot water, was shown by "Vaseline" to my room.

It is curious to hear some of the names bestowed in baptism upon the children by their parents, whose right to so name them is unquestionable.

A clergyman once was requested to christen twins by the names of Wray and Nephew.

He hesitated. "Where did you hear of these names?" he asked, for, being a total abstainer, he was unacquainted with them.

"On de rum bottle, massa," was the black's reply.

The most pretentious names I heard of were some registered at St Peter's on Ginger Piece Mountain, such as Jetorah Alvira Industry, and Almahene Leminia Delight. In another church register are to be found the following curious combination of names: Caroline Celeste Celestina and Minimima Constantina Kelly.

Those who have read "Tom Cringle's Log" will perhaps remember him sitting at dinner in the home of a prosperous West Indian, and, as one could well believe, ejaculating "By Jupiter!" after some good story.

"You want any tink, sah," came a voice behind his chair; "me tink you call for Jupiter."

Tom's astonishment at "the black baboon" being named after the god of a classic age is still greater when he finds out that a she-baboon of the most unprepossessing type, even in the way of negresses, was familiarly called in the household "Mammy Wenus," and another African slave waiting upon them was known as "Daddy Cupid." "Mammy Wenus and Daddy Cupid! Shades of Homer!" cries the laughter-loving, incorrigible middy.

I found several Americans at dinner, who rather liked this old West Indian home, notwithstanding the fact that one meets with better appointed tables elsewhere. The house was nearly one hundred and fifty years old. The spacious sitting-room was cruciform; the floor, and doors, and staircase were all of polished mahogany. Upstairs a long central corridor ran the length of the house from back to front; into this all the bedrooms on either side led out. There are nice drives amongst the old sugar estates, which, in this part of the island, abound; these form, I suppose, the attraction for the small American colony. One lady informed me she was searching for curious old mahogany furniture, especially old cabinets and cupboards of native work, for mahogany, in the days of Jamaican prosperity, was like gold in the reign of Solomon, and was lavishly employed in the inside decoration of houses; now there is scarcely a mahogany tree on the island.

My experience of our Yankee cousins who flock to these shores to recruit their forces, or, like myself, to avoid the reign of the Ice King, has been varied. No pleasanter companion than a well-bred, well-travelled American would I wish to come across; but there is a class which corresponds to that which we know in England as "bounders," which one "strikes" in Jamaica occasionally. This kind of person knows everything. If *he* bossed the island, instead of the man who has the "misfortune to be the official representative of an effete monarchy," things would be very different. This description of the gubernatorial office I quote from an American magazine article, not long since put into my hands; but as I think it is impossible for a mind trained to respect the traditions of a glorious past, and the events of a not inglorious present, to follow the warped course of democratic opinion, I will charitably overlook the above, which no doubt was penned in a spirit of extravagant patriotism, and quote what this writer says further on concerning the inhabitants, whom he describes as "cheerful and thoroughly courteous, neither slavishly servile, but smiling and civil, gentle and reasonable."

There is one thing, however, which rouses my ire. It is to be seriously taken to task over my pronunciation of my own language by a man, who, with every turn of his tongue, distorts and twists it out of all recognisable kinship to any English known or spoken in Great Britain. A good story was told me of a suggestion made by some original American at a time when John Bull and his Yankee cousins were hardly on speaking terms.

Upholders of the Republic declared it to be a shame that they should even speak the same language as perfidious Albion, and insisted that the English tongue henceforth should cease to exist as the national language of America.

"Say! let them darned Britishers get 'nother lingo kinder like for theirselves!" exclaimed one of these gentry.

Surely Shakespeare and Tennyson would turn in their graves could they hear their immortal lines quoted in the high, shrill voices, too well-known to describe further, of American travellers. English, as spoken at the University of Cambridge, is good enough for me, I tell them.

Notwithstanding, I quite enjoyed meeting many very charming visitors from the States. We laughed together over some of the funny stories one hears of the negroes in Jamaica. One of the most amusing is that told by a clergyman who was new to their customs and manners.

Soon after landing in Jamaica he was called upon to bury an old negro at a settlement called Springfield. The son, a "boy" of about forty years of age, had charge of the funeral arrangements. This son had not been kind to his poor old parents; though they were living in the next yard and sorely in need, the son would not give them a bite of yam to eat. The funeral took place on the spot; first of all, in the house a few sentences from the Bible, then a Psalm, then a short passage of Scripture, and then to the grave near the coffee bushes in the yard.

He proceeded with the service amid strange scenery, the only white man within miles of the place. The service having been read to the end, to the clergyman's surprise the son burst out with—

"Now, boys, in wid de dutty!"

They then asked if they might sing a hymn. They were permitted to do so, and as the parson was ignorant as to the kind of hymns they knew, he told them to start one. The son at once led off with—

> "Come let us join our cheerful songs
> Wid angels round de trone."

The clergyman says he made tracks for his horse, musing over the strange nature of these people. He soon found that the local grave nomenclature is as follows: A coffin is called a "box," the grave a "hole," and the earth "dutty" (dirt).

The proverbs, too, are most amusing.

"Breeze no blow, tree no shake." This is equivalent to ours, "You never see smoke without fire."

"Hab money, hab friends."

"If you lie down wid puppy you get up wid flea."

"Sickness ride horse come; him take foot go away."

"Cunning better dan 'trong."

"Cotton tree ebba so big, little axe cut him."

"Cuss, cuss, no bore hole in me 'kin" (hard words break no bones).

According to their publications, Americans consider Jamaica an ideal place for building up the system after over-exertion. In four days from New York they find themselves in a set of conditions totally different from their daily environment in the States.

"Among the many other advantages possessed by Jamaica," says an American, "as a winter resort, not the least is that the tourist, whose presence and spoor are as the brand of Cain on so many of the natural beauties of the world, is almost unknown."

That it is beneficial to nerves as well as interesting to the visitor he further testifies. Men who have gone there physical wrecks in January have returned gay, jaunty, and full of vigour in February. Nerves soon learn to resume their normal functions and cease to torture; sleeplessness is something to laugh at.

I do not know anything more instructive or offering greater inducement to indulge in reveries of bygone times than some of the parish churches of this island. Notably so does the handsome, spacious edifice built of stone in Queen Anne style, at Montego Bay, produce that effect upon the thoughtful observer. Two crimson-blossomed, lofty, flamboyant trees stand like guarding sentries over the pathway leading up to the church. As you pass along, handsome tombs, some with railings round, others being heavy grave-stones with which one is familiar at home, but all bearing traces of the usage of time, lie scattered on either side. Once inside the church and your eye lights on name after name on the mural tablets on the walls which strikes you as familiar. These are generally monuments to the memory of wealthy landowners in times past who possessed the much-coveted sugar estates in the surrounding district, and where indeed their direct or collateral descendants are at the present day it would probably be painful to discover; but before a perfect masterpiece of the sculptor's art I stood literally spell-bound. This is one of Bacon's monuments, bearing the date 1794, and is the far-famed one dedicated to the memory of Rose Palmer. There are two stories connected with this; a local legend, which on the face of it is incorrect, declared that it was erected to a Rose Palmer, a virago famous for her misdeeds, having during her lifetime disposed of four husbands. She was finally murdered by her slaves, whom she had treated with savage cruelty. There is a discoloration around the neck of the figure, and some fancy a mark on the pedestal faintly resembling a blood-stain; these are believed by local superstition to have appeared shortly after the monument was placed *in situ*, manifesting unquestionably her guilt. The rector of Montego Bay, however, told me the correct version. The sculpture represents a most beautifully-moulded female figure gracefully draped, and drooping pathetically over a funereal urn; she is presumably the embodiment of human grief; upon the face of the urn a medallion portraying the features of Rose, the first wife of John Palmer, is seen. The wretch to whose memory this monument has been wrongly ascribed by those who like a good story was an Irish girl, who acted as maid to the first wife, and after her decease became the second Mrs Palmer.

A quaint inscription records the sorrows of the husband who had this beautiful work of art executed in England, to be erected to the memory of a much-beloved wife:

"Her manners were open, cheerful, and agreeable,
And being blessed with a plentiful fortune
Hospitality dwelt with her as long as health permitted her

> to enjoy society.
> Educated by the anxious care of a Reverend
> Divine, her father,
> Her charities were not ostentatious, but of a
> nobler kind.
> She was warm in her attachment to her friends,
> And gave the most signal proof of it
> In the last moments of her life."
> "This tribute of affection and respect
> Is erected by her husband the Honourable John
> Palmer
> as a monument of her worth
> and of his gratitude."

The history of the handsome, but cruel and wanton successor of this gentle lady is significant of the times in which she lived, when the plantation owners had the power of life and death and of bodily mutilation in their hands. In addition to her depraved morals, it is recorded of her that she tortured her girl-slaves by making them wear shoes having wooden soles, which were charged with blunted pegs, and which must have hurt them cruelly when they had to stand upon them. She also beat them with a perforated platter that drew blood. This fiend, presumably from a fit of intense jealousy, caused the death of a beautiful coloured girl, who was the mistress of her stepson. It is said she had her victim led out to be strangled in the presence of all the slaves on the plantation. Afterwards, her head was severed from her body, and Mrs Palmer had it preserved in spirits!

CHAPTER XVII

DESCRIPTION OF ROSE HALL– SUGAR–THE EXPENSE OF WORKING AN ESTATE A CENTURY AGO–BANANA CULTIVATION

The mountains round Montego Bay were the scene of a long and unrelenting struggle between the forces of the government and the Maroons. After a prolonged struggle blood-hounds from Cuba were imported to hunt them down. Many ghastly scenes took place in the recesses and defiles amongst the hills.

I had myself a curious experience in the old West Indian-built house of Miss Harrison, which I give for as much as it is worth; the psychologist might be able to interpret it with satisfaction to himself. I was going up to bed on Sunday evening, and I have mentioned before how handsomely the house was internally fitted up with mahogany stairs, flooring and doors, when I distinctly heard the sound of a crack of a whip immediately in my vicinity. I instinctively turned round to see who was coming up behind me, expecting to see a man with a riding-whip in his hand. Needless to say, there was nobody; it was a moonlight night, and the dim glimmer of a paraffin lamp shone across the landing from some half-open door. I had not been thinking or talking of the history of Jamaican families in years past. Instead, I remember feeling irritated at the fulsome boasting of some of the Americans I had just left.

My hostess was anxious that I should drive out to Rose Hall, the home of the Palmers, whose monument I have described. I think a visit to this house, notwithstanding its dilapidated and ruinous state, is useful, in that one can gain an idea of the wealth and luxuriant mode of living of the estate owners in times when sugar fetched any price between £50 and £70 a ton, instead of its present price, which is about £5. These were the days when fine roads were built, handsome houses such as Rose Hall were erected, and lands brought into cultivation. An almost unbroken girdle of sugar-fields encircled the island. When, however, philanthropic effort, headed by Wilberforce, successfully passed the Emancipation Act, which provided that from and after the 1st of August 1834, all slaves in the colonial possessions of Great Britain should be for ever free, with an intermediate state of four and six years, the condition of the sugar-planters was lamentable. They were left with old machinery, scarcity of labour, and poor markets. Indignation was rife, and they threatened to transfer their allegiance to the United States of America. The immediate results of emancipating negroes from slavery has been practically the same everywhere. After the adoption of free trade many of the estates were simply abandoned, or sold for next to nothing. Probably those who could have foreseen how the fruit trade would eventually supersede sugar, would have clung to their lands at all costs.

To give my readers some idea of the interior of a planter's house in the eighteenth century, I quote from a journal of the Institute of Jamaica a description of the Palmer mansion built for £30,000 in 1760, and richly furnished: "A gap through the boundary wall leads to an avenue of trees, selected for their beauty and fragrance from the endless variety which luxuriates in a southern clime. There may still be seen the cocoa, with its fringy leaves always graceful and always beautiful; the quaint cotton, the king of the forest, from whose huge limbs countless streamers of parasitical plants hang pendent exposed to the breeze; the palm, with its slender speckle of most delicate green; the spreading mahogany, with its small leaves of the deepest dye; and there may be found the ever-bearing orange, with its golden fruit and flowers of rich perfume. Neglect, too, has been here, and the avenue once so trim and neat is now overgrown with weeds and bushes, so much so that the remainder of the ancient wall can scarce now be seen.

"Passing about a half mile through the grove you come suddenly in front of a stately large stone mansion, prettily situated on the top of a gentle slope. The first thing that strikes you is its size and magnitude, the next, the imposing appearance of the flight of steps leading to the main entrance of the mansion. These are 14 feet high, built of large square stone (hewn), and so arranged that the landing-place serves as a portico 20 feet square. A few brass stanchions, curiously wrought and twisted, serve to show what the railing had been, but the few remaining are tarnished with verdigris and broken, bruised and turned in every direction. Magnificent, massive folding-doors of solid mahogany, 4 inches thick, with panels formed by the carver's chisel in many a scroll and many a device, are upheld by brazen hinges which, fashioned like sea-monsters, seem to bite the posts on which they hang. These doors are in front of the main hall, a room of lofty dimensions and magnificent proportions, 40 feet long, 30 wide, 18 feet high, formed of the same costly materials as the doors, carved in the same manner out of solid planks and fashioned in curious and antique forms, while the top is ornamented with a very deep cornice formed after the arabesque pattern. The floor is of the same highly polished wood. Three portraits in richly carved frames and painted by a master-hand immediately attract attention. One of these portraits represents a hard and stern-featured man clothed in the scarlet and ermine robes of a judge. Another is of a mild, benevolent-looking, gentlemanly person, dressed in the fashion of the olden times with powdered hair, lace cravat, ruffles and silk stockings, buckles, brocaded vest and velvet coat. The third is a female of about six-and-twenty, and, if the painter has not flattered her, she must have been of exquisite beauty."

Sugar is talked, and has been talked *ad nauseam* in Jamaica. In one of the leading organs of the Jamaican press I read, in this first week of March 1903, that according to the latest reports from New York the sugar industry is looking up, an appreciable rise in the price of crystals is announced, and this, it is believed, will cause a certain increase in the price of the lower grades of sugar as well. One rejoices to hear that the refiners of sugar in America are beginning to be nervous, lest, in consequence of the coming abolition of the Continental bounty-fed system, the British West Indian sugar should find its way to the markets of the mother-country. There is a special cane called the Muscovados which to the American refineries is indispensable, and which apparently comes in greater bulk from our colonies. In addition, the Brazil crops are not so plentiful as they have been. This being so, there seem to be ample grounds for the hope entertained that the prospects of the sugar industry of this part of the Empire are heightening considerably. Alluding to their hope that in the future there is promise of higher prices generally for cane-sugars, and also to the development and increased outputs of the fruit trade, the writer concludes a most encouraging article with the belief that, all things taken into consideration, Jamaica may be said to be on the eve of a great agricultural and industrial boom.

Now the cultivation of sugar on a large scale implies the circulation of huge sums of money. But those who confidently talk about its revival, and who think that as soon as the bounties are abolished the country will leap back into its former prosperity, forget a very important item on the programme. Certain soils only produce sugar profitably. The area most suitable for the cultivation of cane as a staple article of commerce is a limited one. Westmoreland, Trelawny, and St Thomas, are the parishes where sugar pays for growing because of their proximity to ports. In these days of keen competition, every mile of carriage means so much out of the profits.

I find from a statement supplied by the Merchants' Exchange that the total export of sugar from 1st April 1902 to 10th January 1903 was 13,468 tons, against 11,523 exported during the same period in the preceding year.

The beautiful and verdant green of the waving cane-fields is one of the most beautiful and characteristic sights of the island; the cane grows from 4 to 7 feet high, occasionally it attains a height of 12 feet. The old mills were worked either by water, wind, or cattle. The machinery used for squeezing the juice out of the sugar-cane consisted of three upright iron-plated rollers, or cylinders, 30 to 40 feet in height. The middle one, to which the moving power was applied, turned the other two by means of cogs. Between these rollers the canes previously cut short were twice compressed. Having passed through the first and second rollers they were turned round the middle one by a circular piece of framework, or screen, called the dumb returner, forced back through the second and third, which squeezed them perfectly dry. The cane-juice was received into a leaden bed, and then conveyed into a vessel called the receiver; the refuse cane-trash was used for fuel to boil the liquor. The juice ordinarily contains eight pints of water, one pint of sugar, one pint of oil and mucilaginous gum, with a portion of essential oil.

OLD-FASHIONED SUGAR MILL.

A mill worked by cattle was considered satisfactory if it passed sufficient canes in an hour to yield from 300 to 350 gallons of juice. As the cane-juice ferments so easily, canes must be ground as soon as they are cut, and great care requires to be exercised in throwing aside those which are tainted.

Bryan Edwards sketches the expenses and profits of a sugar estate in the years 1781 to 1791, and I think it will be interesting to unearth it out of his capacious history, which I confess without reserve to be my happy hunting-ground for reliable information concerning Jamaica's eventful past.

He divides the necessary outlay under three heads those of (1) Lands; (2) Building; (3) Stock.

(1.) Lands.

To buy 600 acres of land	£8,400	0	0
Clearing 300 and planting it at £12 per acre	3,600	0	0
Enclosing and fencing altogether	700	0	0
Clearing and planting 100 acres with provisions	700	0	0
Clearing and planting 100 acres with guiney-grass	700	0	0
TOTAL (in Jamaica currency)	£14,100	0	0

(2.) Buildings.

Water or cattle mills, boiling-house and fittings, curing-house and fittings, overseer's house, trash houses, hospital, prison for negroes, mule stables, shops, sheds, utensils (Jamaica currency)	£7,000	0	0

(3.) Stock.

260 negroes, 80 steers, 60 mules	£20,380	0	0

Lands	£14,100	0	0
Buildings	7,000	0	0
Stock	20,380	0	0
TOTAL (Jamaica currency)	£41,480	0	0
(English sterling)	£30,000	0	0

The produce of such a plantation at the London markets, 1781-1791, he reckons thus:—

	Sterling.		
200 hogsheads of sugar	£3,000	0	0
130 puncheons of rum	1,300	0	0
Gross returns	£4,300	0	0

The net returns, after sundry necessary disbursements, he gives as 7 per cent. on a capital of £30,000.

I was enabled to go over a rum factory, perhaps one of the best known in the island: Appleton rum finds its best market in Jamaica, and is not exported at all. In this case the rum is made from the whole of the cane instead of from the molasses or skimmings of the boiling fluid.

Some of the tourists whom I met had driven from the quaint little town of Falmouth to Montego Bay, a distance of 24 miles along the coast. They were charmed with the beautiful views, especially the grand sunset as they approached Montego Bay; and I do not think I have ever seen more lovely colouring anywhere than here where the exquisitely soft tints seem to melt into each other. The Government is waking up seriously to the fact that the harbour of Falmouth should be improved, and the people of Trelawny have voiced their grievances to some tune since £12,000 are to be spent in deepening the channel.

The Hon. L. C. Shirley, at the last meeting of the Parochial Board, very emphatically urged the need of shipping facilities. He had seen in the days of sugar prosperity five or six barques in the harbour at one time, but, said he, "Sugar and rum being at their lowest ebb, something else must be done. Bananas meant money, but if we have no facilities for shipping what would be the good of planting?"

One of the best authorities in the island on agricultural possibilities and prospects informed me, not long since, that there were old sugar estates to be bought in the neighbourhood of Falmouth for a mere song, which, if purchased now that there is the certainty of improving the harbour, would in a year or so return 100 per cent. if turned into banana plantations. I rather wished I were a man with a capital of £2,000, but when I asked if banana-growing required much experience—

"Yes," said he, "A young fellow should get on a banana estate for a year at least, before laying out his capital."

"It is a matter of learning which soil is particularly adapted," I suggested.

"Not only that," he rejoined, "but an inexperienced man has no idea how to manage his labourers, and there are always sharks ready to take advantage of his ignorance."

Which latter I knew to be sapient wisdom, from the unhappy experience of a youthful relative whose gullibility was apparent to an antipodean swindler, with the result that the sorrow-stricken youth learnt wisdom at the expense of a lightened purse.

There is nothing chimerical in the success of the banana trade. America statistically absorbs most of this produce. On all sides we hear of the variety of ways it is useful as an article of diet, whilst its nutritive powers are unquestioned.

America largely buys banana flour. In its unripe stages it is more properly a vegetable. Green bananas mashed and eaten like potatoes form most useful food, whilst ripe bananas, dried and put up in boxes like figs, are both wholesome and satisfying. From the 1st of April 1902 to 10th January 1903, 90,204,597 bunches of bananas were exported from Jamaica.

In the lowlands, where the climate is hot and moist, bananas are at their best. In preparing ground to grow them the land is ploughed with eight or ten oxen, and the plants are put in from 10 to 15 feet apart. The height they attain is a matter of soil and cultivation. At the end of the first year a crop is ready to be gathered. Each plant produces one bunch only. The plants send out suckers from their roots, which are allowed to grow. Thus, when the first plant is cut down as worthless, another is ready to bear; others are in different stages of growth. This goes on for about seven years, when it is needful to plough again and replant the ground in some places, but I have been told of the same banana-trees remaining in bearing thirty and forty years. As the price fluctuates, it has not the element of certainty that coffee has.

CHAPTER XVIII
MONEAGUE HOTEL—THE TROUBLES OF CHRISTOPHER COLUMBUS

Returning from Montego Bay, I went by rail to Ewarton, which is in the centre of Jamaica. To go there I had to change at Spanish Town, which is 10 miles or so from Kingston. There is only one train every day that runs the whole distance from Montego Bay to Kingston; this starts at eight o'clock in the morning, stopping at every station, and reaches its destination about four in the afternoon. On this occasion I fell in with a number of the island clergy, who entered the train at every stopping-place, several having driven distances of 25 and 30 miles, having risen before daybreak. Since most of the cocks in Jamaica are different from their feathered kindred of other climes, and keep up one unhallowed chorus of crowing all through the night, it is not a great difficulty to tear yourself from your couch.

They were on their way to attend the yearly Synod, which holds its meetings every January, or, as in this case, February. I met my new acquaintance, the rector of Montego Bay, in the train. He told me he had been over twenty years in Jamaica, and he was, I should say, a man of about forty-five years of age.

"But you have been home of course several times in those years?" I questioningly asked him.

"Not a bit of it, Madam," was his curt rejoinder. Apparently he was in the best of health, and had, to my knowledge, taken four services without assistance the day previous, which was Sunday, that I never imagined for a moment it was possible to keep so much vitality and energy going without occasional recruiting sea-voyages and change from this enervating climate.

"How do you think I look?" asked he, slapping his chest, and drawing himself up to his full height, which was not beyond that of the average male adult.

"Very fit," was my reply.

"Go home and tell them what a man can look like out here, after twenty years of total abstinence, and never going home once in all that time." A mischievous gleam shot from his eyes as he spoke.

"How many services did you take yesterday?" I asked him.

"An early celebration and a baptism before I met you." This had been about half-past nine in the morning, when I was sitting on one of the crazy tombs in the churchyard, with my attention divided between the sketch I had been making and my dread of being walked over by a huge spider, or chance scorpion, to say nothing of occasional futile attempts to thin the mosquito life of the island, for they always pestered me so when sketching that I had no conscientious scruples as to massacring them mercilessly.

"Yes," I said; "then you had a second celebration after the eleven o'clock service, and you preached a good twenty minutes."

"Did you time me?" I laughed. "Well!" continued he, "I had a children's service in the afternoon, and evensong at six, so you will admit I had a fairly busy day."

"What a pity they don't send out our curates to do a good ten years in the colonies before giving them livings in England!"

I exclaimed, thinking of some of the weaklings who complained of being overworked at home. Our conversation drifted to other topics. I said the black race struck me as being nothing more than grown-up children, and he agreed that that was the best way of regarding them. He told me of the reduced circumstances which some families owning, formerly, large estates had fallen into; this, according to him, being the result of reckless extravagance, and never putting aside for a rainy day.

"They must have had splendid incomes," I commented.

"There's no doubt of it," assented he.

"What *did* they spend their money on?" I asked, thinking of the hundred and one ways, nowadays, in which money flies, and of the really few amusements that would present themselves in the middle of the eighteenth century to these planters.

"Themselves," he answered, without hesitation; "in luxuriant living, in dress, and in having a good time at home."

Before Spanish Town was reached, I met some persons whom I had seen previously at Mandeville, and we drove together from Ewarton Station over Mount Diabolo, which is 2000 feet above sea-level, and from whence most exquisite views are to be obtained over St Thomas in the vale. This is one of the best drives in the island, and certainly should not be missed. The Moneague Hotel is a very spacious and comfortable building; it stands on a hill, and before you turn up towards it, a huge cotton-tree, with the longest spurs I ever saw, stands in the centre of a pasture, extending its gaunt limbs from its huge truck as a terrestrial octopus might be supposed to do. I went up to Moneague especially to visit this part of the country, which is perfectly lovely whichever way you go. The day following my arrival I took a forty-mile drive. A most entertaining coloured man acted in the capacity of coachman, and as we drove along in a one-seated buggy drawn by a pair of strong ponies, he told me the names of those trees with which I was not acquainted. I faintly suspected in one or two cases he drew upon his imagination: he did not answer quite so glibly as he had done previously. We passed very fine grazing estates, and I gathered from my loquacious informer that some persons in the island had made very fair fortunes through grazing and cattle-rearing. The chief charm of this long day was the road leading through Fern Gully down to the small town of Ora Cabessa, on the north side of the island. You drive between enormously high cliffs covered with every variety of fern; the moisture and shade causes their growth to be quite gigantic, and you look up to the bit of blue sky overhead through the interlacing and waving greenery of countless tropical plants. On emerging from the Gully you arrive at Ora Cabessa, where a police-station, a post-office, and a telegraph-station acquaint you with the fact that you are once more in the haunts of civilisation. Here groves of cocoa-nut-trees bend almost down to the water's edge, and the coast scenery is lovely. Ochos Rios, meaning "eight rivers," is a little further on.

In the vicinity are the two waterfalls made by the Roaring River in its course to the sea; the lower is very pretty, but the fall a mile higher up in private property is well worth seeing. Here a more villainous breed of ticks seems to abound, for everyone warns you to beware of them, and several men we met on the road who had visited the falls, were diligently inspecting their nether garments; they were what the native contemptuously calls "walkfoot buckra," as distinguished from "carriage buckra." There are many funny nigger sayings which, the longer one lives in Jamaica, the more one grasps their significance. "To a dog's face say Mr Dog, behind his back Dog," is one of them. Substitute for the dog the white man, and you have learnt a fundamental truth.

I was told by my coloured coachman that no native will wear cast-off clothing. Another thing that interested me, as pertaining to the native folk-lore, was the reverence in which children hold spiders. They will curtsey to them, talk to them on their way to school. Some persons say this is the last vestige of some old African totem-worship connected with this insect. I have not mentioned the land crabs which abound at these waterfalls. The natives call them "soldiers"; they are quite harmless, and I have heard that they are eaten by the blacks.

I cannot turn my back on this lovely northern coast without alluding to the ever-memorable landing of the great Columbus, which happened in 1504, during his fourth journey to the New World near this spot. He had discovered the highlands of Jamaica in 1494, and in the united names of Ferdinand and Arragon had taken possession of it. A devout Catholic, he could do no otherwise than obey the decree of Pope Alexander VI. to the effect that "omnes insulas et terras firmas inventas et inveniendas, detectas et detegendas versus Occidentem" were given to the Spanish Crown.

It is sorrowful reading which tells us how, suffering from base ingratitude, in tempestuous weather, and with much difficulty, he reached a haven since known as Don Christopher's Cove, on the north side of the island, with two crippled and leaking ships, which he ran aground to prevent their foundering. He quite made up his mind to die there. His crews revolted, the Indians deserted him, the Governor of Hispaniola mocked his misfortunes. In much suffering, and amongst his rebellious countrymen, he writes to the King of Spain, and says how low "his zeal for the service of King Ferdinand and his mistress Queen Isabella had brought him, how his men who were in health mutinied under Poras of Seville." He adds: "As my misery makes my life a burthen to myself, so I fear the empty title of Vice-Roy and Admiral render me obnoxious to the hatred of the Spanish nation.

"It is visible that all methods are adopted to cut the thread that is breaking, for I am in my old age oppressed with insupportable pains of the gout, and am now languishing and expiring with that and other infirmities among savages, when I have neither medicines nor provisions for the body, priest nor sacrament for the soul. My men in a state of revolt, my brother, my son, and those that are faithful, sick, starving, and dying. Let it not bring a further infamy on the Castilian name, nor let future ages know that there were wretches so vile in this, that think to recommend themselves to Your Majesty by destroying the unfortunate and miserable Christopher Columbus." In conclusion, he pathetically appeals to Queen Isabella: "She, if she lives, will consider that cruelty and ingratitude will bring down the wrath of Heaven, so that the wealth I have discovered shall be the means of stirring up all mankind to revenge and rapine, and the Spanish nation suffer hereafter, for what envious, malicious, and ungrateful people do now."

The Spaniards brought their priests over with them when they took possession of the island. The religious ceremonies were conducted in handsome edifices, although no traces remain of them. At the first capital, Seville D'oro, founded by Diego, the discoverer's son, a collegiate church was built. In 1688 the founder of the British Museum declared that there were ruins of ecclesiastical buildings at Seville, which were situated near the modern St Ann's Bay, but all such remains have long since passed away with the increased agriculture and the rapid growth of tropical flora. No one seems able to tell why the Spaniards changed their seat of government in 1530, from Seville D'oro to St Jago de la Vega, the modern Spanish town, where an abbey, churches, and chapels were built.

I returned to Moneague *viâ* Claremont. The road ascends for a long distance through fine estates; it is well graded, and, looking back, lovely peeps of the sea are afforded. At the top of the hill it is well to leave the carriage and climb up on a gate or wall, when an extended coast scene, including St Ann's Bay, is visible. A pretentious little fruit-boat, busy as a honey-bee, was puffing away towards Ora Cabessa, where she anchored, for the coast is too shallow at most of the ports where the ships call for fruit to allow of their coming alongside the wharf. The sea was an exquisite blue, and a band of bright green cane-fields bordered the coast, whilst pimento-trees and cocoa-nut groves waved in the distance.

I told the driver to be merciful to his beast up that long hill. I was tired, I said, and had come a long journey the day previously. When I told him I had come from Montego Bay to the hotel, he expressed surprise that I was able to take so long a drive as that we were going.

"Ladies 'bout yar would go to bed after a journey like dat, and not rise up again till de turd day."

I told him Englishwomen were able to endure much greater hardships than West Indian ladies.

"Did I not want a coachman to take back with me?" he asked. He would so much like to go to England. A little further conversation, and I elicited from him he had a weak lung. That, I said, put that matter completely out of the question. If in Jamaica his lungs were weak, he would not live a month in our colder climate. That seemed to upset his calculations.

"Besides, you would not like the food," I told him. "We have not half the good things at home you have here." And we fell to discussing foods.

"Give a man out yar salt-fish and akee and roasted bread-fruit far breakfast, and he trow away all de ham and eggs into de street," said he.

We met some desperately poor, ill-clad negroes, and I asked if they were not very idle.

"No, missus; they can't get work to do. They don't know how to do any ting properly for to get any money. Some of dem don't earn eight dollars in a whole year," he added.

I reckoned up eight dollars as not quite two pounds, and felt aghast at that for a living wage. The driver had all unwittingly put his finger upon a sore spot in the educational policy of Jamaica. The present generation are mostly too grand to work with their hands as their parents did before them. They connect domestic service and work with slavery, and every girl who has a smattering of knowledge wants to be a school-teacher or a dressmaker. The next generation, it is to be hoped, will not be educated above their position in life, then existence in Jamaica for white women may cease to be the harrowing anxiety it seems to be at present. We are not ignorant of the difficulties of housekeeping at home, with a class of women-servants who are not trained to work, and who are neither reliable or conscientious, but, with the thickheadedness of the black thrown in, the case is much worse out here.

COCOA-NUT GROVE.

I will not conclude this chapter without alluding to the cultivation of the cocoa-nut palm-tree. Owing to the long time it is necessary to wait for the first crop, not so much has been done in growing this tree. It seldom bears until seven years old, but when once it is in good bearing, it goes on for a hundred years. The yield of a tree averages one hundred nuts yearly; the bright green blossom and the ripe fruit appear simultaneously. The cocoa-nut palm grows best near the sea, but does not require such rich, moist soil as the banana. The rule is that as soon as the tops are out of reach, the land on which they grow can be put into pasture. The nut is mostly harvested before it is quite ripe. Cocoa-nut milk is made from gratings of the kernel. They carve the shell, and it serves many purposes. The dried kernel is known as "kopra," and is boiled down for the preparation of oil. The solid fat is made into candles, and the oil is used for cooking and for lamps. The cake which is left, or "poonac," is a good food for cattle, also used as a manure. The husk of the fruit yields a fibre which is made into cordage, nets, etc. The tender leaves are made into mats and boxes, the mature into matting, sails, etc. The ash yields potash. The midribs of the leaflets are converted into brooms and brushes; the stalk of the spadix into brushes for whitewashing. Other parts are also useful.

CHAPTER XIX
WOMEN'S RIGHTS IN JAMAICA—A BREAKDOWN OF THE RAILWAY—PORT ANTONIO—CHESTER VALE

Returning to Kingston I took up my quarters for a short time at Myrtle Bank Hotel. A delicious sea-breeze cooled the air during the daytime, whilst at night one could sleep better than at many hotels where I have stayed. One I know of is intensely noisy. Just when you are falling off to sleep some person in the next room violently thrusts open his door and shies his boots down the corridor, instead of quietly putting them outside, then shuts it with a bang, without a moment's consideration of the fact that other persons may be disturbed by the might of his biceps; this, with the incessant crowing of cocks and barkings of dogs occasionally makes night hideous to contemplate.

Whilst here, I took the opportunity of attending one or two of the meetings of the Anglican Synod.

The disestablishment of the Church of England in Jamaica took place some thirty years ago; but as I intend to give a slight sketch of the ecclesiastical history of the island in my next chapter, I will content myself with saying that the subject to be discussed was, whether the women who, as registered members, subscribe their weekly pence to the maintenance of the church much better than do the male portion, were to be allowed the privilege of voting for the officials of their separate churches.

One venerable archdeacon, whose trite speech and characteristic physiognomy is well known in this town, waxed most eloquent upon the virtues of the "enfranchised she." Another worthy, with an equal love of justice, declared that "but for the women, the churches could not exist in Jamaica," and said it was simply justice to give them a voice in their church representation. The result of the meeting was, however, to postpone the measure for a more convenient occasion; it was thought inadvisable to rush it upon the native ladies; in the meanwhile they could gradually be educated up to a more extended view of their interests and privileges. Thus, even the weaker sex in this far-off island of the Caribbean Sea has been touched with a ripple from the wave which bears on its crest the emancipation of women from the fetters and gyves man, from the beginning of the world, encumbered the object of his adoration.

To-day, in enlightened England, might instead of right is still to the fore directly the question is one of giving woman her undoubted rights. Man is the same inconsequent reasoner. When he finds a woman cannot assimilate, or apply what she has learnt so quickly as he can himself, he ofttimes forgets the shallow education he thought good enough for her, though probably the sons were sent to the university, and he irritably reproaches her with the fact of her sex, for which she is not responsible, and her frivolity, for which latter, not having chosen to spend money over her education, he is distinctly to blame.

If she educates herself, and has a mind of her own, and finds words to express her views which do not always coincide with his own, he sneers at her for being a blue-stocking, and declares no man wants an opinionated wife.

The most curious anomalies exist. Women doctors, lecturers, teachers, clerks, telegraphists, business women, and those who administer their own estates, are denied by our enlightened and liberal-minded legislators the privilege of voting for parliamentary representation, thereby placing them on the same level as the pauper and the lunatic, who, I believe, are the only classes of unenfranchised male adults. Surely women who pay taxes might be considered capable of voting for the legislators of their country.

I had heard and read a good deal of Port Antonio, and intended visiting the place. Hearing some friends were going, I agreed to go with them.

We left Kingston at two in the afternoon, and should have reached Port Antonio at six in the evening, in good time for dinner, intending to take either a moonlight stroll or drive afterwards.

The first part of the journey occurred without mishap. We were just half-way, and it was after four o'clock, when, apparently, we were making an extra long stay at a station. Several passengers grumbled, peered out, then discovered something had gone wrong with the works. This is of such everyday occurrence that nobody seemed alarmed. In a few moments we learnt, quite casually, that a luggage train was derailed in a tunnel 200 yards ahead, and as it was a single line to Port Antonio, we should probably wait some time before we could proceed.

We must have waited at that God-forsaken spot nearly two hours. There was no inn or habitation where we could get as much as a cup of tea! We were then told to re-enter the train, which would take us to the entrance of the tunnel. We would have then to walk through to the other end, where a train was now waiting to take us to our destination. It was growing dark; the train crawled cautiously down a fairly steep incline, until both engines faced each other, only about 20 or 30 yards being left between them. The luggage was transferred, and we commenced our subterranean walk.

As we passed the derailed engine, which presented a slightly drunken aspect, the heat of the tunnel, combined with that from the roaring and steaming locomotive, was thoroughly appalling; at the same time the shouting of the officiate and the chattering of the blacks, who, laden with baggage, pushed past, made one think one had "struck" the direct road to the infernal regions. Only a narrow, stony footway between the rails and the wall of the tunnel made progress a matter of difficulty.

We were nearly exhausted when we once more emerged into the twilight. The train lingered at every stopping-place; it was dark, so we could not see the north coast. Instead of six, it was eleven at night when at last we lumbered into Port Antonio.

We had had neither bite nor sup since one o'clock, and were fairly famished. To add to our misfortunes, it was raining in torrents at Port Antonio; no conveyance was at the station. A messenger was promptly despatched to the hotel for a "bus." In about twenty minutes a couple of buggies drove up in the darkness, and whirled us up a steep hill to the only establishment the town possesses, where we arrived nearly dead-beat with fatigue. We instantly clamoured for brandy, or whisky and soda, but found, to our dismay, that it was a temperance hotel! I fear we reviled the upholders of that noble cause, but there was nothing to be done but swallow cold, weak tea, and stay our hunger on the uninviting scraps of meat they brought us with much grumbling. Giving us any food at all was evidently a work of supererogation on their part. We represented that ours was an exceptional case, but it is well to learn that the American who intends to make dollars, and plenty of them, has no time for politeness, nor is there room in his policy for the milk of human kindness.

This was my introduction to the much-lauded American establishment known as the Tichfield Hotel, which I had heard spoken of as the best hotel in the island. It certainly is beautifully situated on a hill overlooking the harbour, and the fruit, which is lavishly set before the visitor at every meal, is quite a feature. The building is commodious, and cleanliness and comfort are decidedly not lacking.

The sea-bathing here is good and safe, being protected from the sea by a coral reef, over which the waves dash majestically—a lovely sight as seen from the verdure-clad hills. The temperature of the water is about 80°. The Americans who patronise it come direct here in the United Fruit Company's steamers from Philadelphia and New York. In fact, the hotel is run by that Company, and at the time of writing these lines (March 1903) there is not sufficient accommodation in the town for the numbers arriving from the States. This is distinctly satisfactory; the fruit-growing in the neighbourhood—for many old sugar estates are now owned by Americans—has changed the condition of the country from depression into prosperity, which one fervently hopes may be still more increased.

That our cousins on the other side of the Atlantic appreciate the island scenery is evident; those I have met in various parts have rapturously extolled its beauties, whilst they have taken sorely to heart the low state of Jamaican finance. An American magazine has an article in which the writer remarks upon the island inhabitants most favourably; he alludes in warm terms to their native courtesy and good-nature, their smiling civility and gentleness. Comparing the behaviour of Jamaican youths with that of his youthful countrymen, he writes: "We occasionally invite eminent foreign educationalists over here to teach us how to teach. If a hundred young Jamaicans could be invited to teach pupils of public schools how to study and how to behave, we could expect striking results."

PORT ANTONIO.

He is conscious of the reputation of his compatriots for lack of breeding and good manners, for he deprecates that feeling amongst the American colonists of this town and its environs, which made them manifest unwillingness to show civility to the Governor of Jamaica when visiting Port Antonio. It is amusing to read that the fact remains that no ill-bred person, no matter what his nationality, is bound to be civil to anybody; and surely if an ordinary, not to say common, American citizen at home may with impunity run down the President of the United States and then be studiedly impertinent to him, a travelling American may be allowed to rise in wrath at the thought of being polite to a British Governor!

However *blasé* the globe-trotter may be, it is impossible for him not to be moved by the tropical beauty and restfulness of this spot as a winter resort; the exquisite colouring of the sea, the white surf nearer to you, the green verdure of the hills around, and the towering of majestic waving palms unite to form this a charming retreat for jaded nerves.

Many persons in returning to Kingston leave the train at Annotto Bay, having beforehand ordered a carriage to be in readiness, and drive to Castleton Gardens, a distance of 12 miles. These are botanical grounds, and well worth the visit; part of them are situated on a river, where the cool shade of bamboo arbours forms a pleasant resting-place for lunch. Then a further distance of 14 miles or so brings you across the island to Constant Spring Hotel.

I was now desirous of making my last excursion into the mountains. Many a time I had gazed longingly at the Blue Mountain Peak and Catherine Peak, and I now arranged to stay some days at the coffee plantation of Mr Sidgwick, Chester Vale, situated nearer the latter mountain.

I was told at the Myrtle Bank Hotel that the ride up was fairly steep and would occupy three hours; but any qualms as to one's powers of endurance were stifled at birth, when I learnt that an aged lady, of probably seventy, contemplated taking the journey with me. I had met her in various parts of the island, invariably grumbling at the non-existence of electric light and other trifles. She should have remained at home, many of us thought. For people of that age to attempt to travel in an island so remote, and as yet so barely furnished with good hotels, is preposterous; they are a terror to those who can get along very well without their company, which, at best, is an onerous responsibility. In this case, I wondered what I should do if the old lady fell off her horse in a fit of apoplexy, for it was excessively hot, and the places we climbed up were enough to try an experienced rider.

We took the electric tram, first of all, from the hotel to Papine, some 6 miles in an eastward direction. Here, by the bye, there is a black Lourdes. I did not see the dirty pool where a crazed enthusiast, a black man, named Bedward, holds forth as to the miraculous nature of the water, and where faith-healing is carried on *à merveille*. Negroes having cancers, tumours, and other ailments go there and wash. The accompanying rites I do not know, for the proceedings take place at night, and therefore it is not easy to be present. But undoubtedly cures have taken place, so greatly does fear, or faith, operate upon the nervous centres of blacks as well as whites. The natives take bottles containing this miraculous water which everybody, no matter what the disease, bathes in, and when a member of their family is sick or ill, he or she is dosed with it. From Papine carriages were in readiness to convey travellers to Gordon Town, some 3 miles of lovely winding road away amongst the hills.

Here we took horses; our luggage was strapped on to a mule's back, and, with a boy in attendance, we commenced our three hours' ride. The way led over bridges through a defile, then leaving the main road we ascended a good bridal path which zigzagged up the face of a very steep mountain affording, as we got up some 3000 feet, magnificent views of the country and harbour of Kingston beneath us. At length we gained the summit of the pass, and then our way led round circuitous mountains with a deep valley between us and another range. All the sturdy mountaineers we passed on the narrow path seemed pleased to see us. Wattled huts, and occasionally a Chinaman's drink shop, were passed; each new view seemed to be more beautiful than the last. At length we gradually descended the hill, crossed a bridge, and immediately ascended the other side of the narrow ravine. Very soon after, entering a gate, we found ourselves in Mr Sidgwick's coffee plantation, which occupied the slope of a very steep hill. Another gate led into the garden of our host, which could boast of a tennis-lawn and terraces. At the back were enormous barbecues and buildings connected with the curing of coffee.

The house itself is two hundred years old, and is situated in a basin amongst the hills. It is built in the mode so prevalent in the older houses of Jamaica, namely, the large central dining-room with rooms and kitchen opening into it, and on the storey above, the drawing-room, with bedrooms leading into it. Going through the house one crossed the roadway, where a billiard-room and a wing containing ten bedrooms were in course of erection, for, in the summer months, there is an exodus to the hills from Kingston, by those who can afford the change. We had fires every night, and a most genial and happy house-party we were, when the grumblesome old dame had departed, playing whist and bridge, and enjoying the treat of a really good piano. The food in these remote regions is excellent, notwithstanding that most of it has to be carried up from Kingston.

I cannot describe the charm of the walks and rides to be taken in this mountainous region. The ascent to Catherine's Peak is by no means arduous, but the path up to the summit is to be found with some difficulty owing to the luxuriant growth of the wild ginger, ferns and other plants. The ever-changing lights on the verdure-clad sides of the Blue Mountains is a wonderful sight for an artistic eye, whilst torrents and streams, hidden by the great masses of trees, ferns, and plants of all description, fall into the narrow valleys. It is only the pedestrian who can fully grasp the great wealth of greenery everywhere. The tree ferns grow to great height amongst the mountains where the sunlight does not penetrate. Wild heliotrope, orchids, wild oleander, begonias, one can pick as one wanders along.

CHAPTER XX

THE CHURCH OF ENGLAND IN JAMAICA—ITS DISESTABLISHMENT, ITS INCREASED ACTIVITY AND DEVELOPMENT

In briefly reviewing the past history, and in contemplating the present state of the Church of England in this colony, there are no words which present themselves to my mind with greater significance than do those of Ruskin. He says: "There are two oriflammes: which shall we plant on the farthest islands?—the one that floats in heavenly fire, or that which hangs heavy with foul tissue of terrestrial gold? We have been taught a religion of pure mercy, which we must now either finally betray, or learn to defend by fulfilling. And we are rich in an inheritance of honour bequeathed to us through a thousand years of noble history." That we have not betrayed that trust in this colony there is ample evidence, and that the bright inheritance of honour remains untarnished, the very existence of an active, flourishing, and self-supporting Church in Jamaica testifies, in spite of the dark days and difficult times it has lived through since its disestablishment in 1870.

To understand the somewhat complicated history of Anglicanism in these parts, it will be profitable to revert to the time when Cromwell, in fitting out the expedition commanded by Penn and Venables to crush the Spanish power in the West Indies in 1655, despatched seven ministers of religion at the same time. That stern Puritan and sound statesman could not brook the overbearing pride of Spain, nor was he inclined to submit to the Spanish pretensions with the tameness with which the vacillating Stuart kings had viewed the policy of aggrandizement pursued by that State. Its maritime power menaced his commerce on the high seas; doubtlessly its very existence troubled his Puritan and mystical conscience.

Whether the expedition which Carlyle speaks of as "the unsuccessfulest enterprise Oliver Cromwell ever had concern with," resulting in our gaining possession of Jamaica, was the outcome of his foreign policy or of religious motives, is not quite clear, but we know that the general who succeeded Venables drew up a formal request, asking that "godly, sober and learned ministers" should be sent out to them, prefacing his request with the words, "Forasmuch as we conceive the propagation of the Gospel was the thing principally aimed and intended in this expedition." Commending General Fortescue for his "faithfulness and constancy in the midst of other's miscarriages," the Protector, alluding to the reproof of God given them in their repulse at St Domingo, characteristically bewails the reports he has received of their avarice, pride, and debauchery, and hopes that a special regard may be so exercised, that virtue and godliness may receive due encouragement, etc.

Whatever zeal for religion the conquerors possessed apparently exhausted itself in iconoclastic outbursts similar to the manner in which the Independents in England earned for themselves immortal obloquy in the mutilation of sacred buildings. Here the victorious soldiers destroyed every Roman Catholic place of worship in the island.

About this time heavy mortality thinned the troops; but the land became repeopled by Cromwell's coercive Irish campaigns. Two thousand men and women were shipped to Jamaica, whilst in Scotland the sheriffs had orders to "apprehend all known idle, masterless rogues and vagabonds, male and female, and transport them to the island." The Spaniards, noting the ravages which sickness was making in the troops of their victors, made a futile attempt to regain the island, but General D'Oyley defeated them in 1658 at Rio Nuevo.

In 1666, with the accession of the Merry Monarch, Lord Windsor took measures for the encouragement of an orthodox ministry. Laws were passed regulating ecclesiastical matters and providing liberally for clerical support, all colonies and plantations being then within the episcopal jurisdiction of the Bishop of London.

In 1681, and afterwards, instructions to successive governors declared that "no minister be received in Jamaica without license from the Right Rev. the Lord Bishop of London." But the Jamaica Assembly, which sat two hundred and two years, appreciating the security at which their distance from Whitehall gave them, were by no means a mild and docile legislative body. The absurdity of not being able to get rid of an undesirable clergyman, without the permission of a bishop residing 4000 miles away, caused the passing of an Act which questioned the right of the Bishop of London to suspend either *ab officio*, or *a beneficio*, from the island.

Thus at the close of the seventeenth century the State Church in Jamaica was firmly established on a legal basis. In a history dealing with ecclesiastical matters of this period, it appears that the Church was regarded by the Assembly who voted the necessary funds for its maintenance as a respectable and ornamental adjunct of the State. Possibly if the clergy had shown great signs of missionary zeal, its very existence would not have been tolerated. Apparently at this date they ministered almost solely to the whites. The legislators who voted supplies were almost all of them planters, therefore slave-owners. They were, one would imagine, sufficiently intelligent to perceive that Christian teaching, if spread amongst the blacks, would inevitably tend to produce discontent and a sense of ill-treatment. Probably they would have sympathised with Lord Melbourne, who, at a later date, accidentally found himself listening to an evangelical sermon, in which sin and its consequences were sternly depicted, when he expressed his disgust in these words: "Things have come to a pretty pass when religion is allowed to invade the sphere of private life." That the condition of the Church in Jamaica was deplorable during the eighteenth century is undoubtedly true, although there were here and there bright examples of a higher standard of life than ordinarily prevailed. In Long's "History," written in 1774, we read that there were seldom wanting some who "were equally respectable for their learning, piety, and exemplary good behaviour, others have been detestable for their drinking, gambling, and iniquity." He further declares that "some labourers of the Lord's vineyard have at times been sent who were much better qualified to be retailers of salt-fish, or boatswains to privateers, than ministers of the Gospel." Another writer, speaking of the clergy, says they were "of a character so vile that I do not care to mention it." Without enlarging further on the wickedness prevailing in Jamaica, it will be but fair to remember what was the tone of society in England at this epoch, and we assuredly do not err when we say that in Georgian times religion had reached its low water-mark.

In the days of Erastianism when a bishop was enthroned by proxy, chosen because he could play a good hand at cards, or because he was bear-leader to some scion of aristocracy, or, like Blomfield or Marsh, good controversialists who could toss a Calvinist, or gore an Evangelical, one could scarcely imagine such worthy successors of the Apostles, as they drove to Court functions (even the most impecunious of them) in their carriages with four horses, or discussed the latest scandal over the port that stocked the episcopal cellars, taking great trouble to select fitting men for curacies in a remote island they were never likely to set foot on.

The low state of morals amongst both clergy and laity in England in the eighteenth century is notorious. The poor were left in a state of ignorance and degradation which, in these days, it is difficult to credit. Decency was scarcely known. Profligacy reigned in the highest circles of society. In Lord Holland's "Memoirs of the Whig Party" we read that at the wedding of the heir-apparent he was so drunk that his attendant dukes could scarcely support him from falling. In Georgian times the conversation and jokes of the first gentlemen in Europe were such that would disgrace a self-respecting stableman in these days, whilst the drinking bouts of the age exceeded anything known in English history previously. Sir George Trevelyan's lines describe the situation so aptly that I cannot refrain from quoting them:

> "We much revere our sires; they
> were a famous race of men.
> For every glass of port we drink,
> they nothing thought of ten.

> They lived above the foulest drains,
> they breathed the closest air,
> They had their yearly twinge of
> gout, but little seemed to care.
> But though they burned their coals at home,
> nor fetched their ice from Wenham,
> They played the man before Quebec
> and stormed the lines at Blenheim.
> When sailors lived on mouldy bread
> and lumps of rusty pork,
> No Frenchman dared to show his nose
> between the Downs and Cork."

The conscience of the British nation slumbered peacefully until at the beginning of the nineteenth century, "in the teeth of clenched antagonisms," the revivalistic preaching of the Evangelicals produced a marked change on religious thought and life: decency once more became fashionable. Extravagance in dress, and in the mode of living, was put down in many of the houses of the great nobles. Clerical iniquities, such as the holding of pluralities, leaving secluded country spots practically heathen, were enquired into and abuses remedied. That the change which had come over the face of things was due to the ghastly tragedies which took place on the other side of the channel, the wholesale slaughter of the French royalty and aristocracy, the tearing up by the roots of all religion and order culminating in the storming of the Bastille by a ferocious mob, is the verdict of no less an authority than Mr Gladstone, who wrote as follows: "I have heard persons of great weight and authority, such as Mr Grenville and also, I think, Archbishop Howley, ascribe the beginnings of a reviving seriousness in the upper classes of lay society to a reaction against the horrors and impieties of the first French Revolution in its later stages." In another passage taken from "The Dinner-bell of the House of Commons," we can feel even to-day how intense the shock must have been throughout the civilised world, and how great the impetus given to mend their ways by the demoniacal proceedings in France: "A voice like the Apocalypse sounded over Europe, and even echoed in all the courts of Europe. Burke poured the vials of his hoarded vengeance into the agitated heart of Christendom, and stimulated the panic of a world by the wild pictures of his inspired imagination."

This was a transitional time in English national life; that it was bloodless may be ascribed to the solid sense and law-abiding temperament of the Anglo-Saxon race. Men like George Eliot's immortal creation, "Edgar Tryan of Milby," battled with the quiescent worldliness of an unenthusiastic episcopate. In the ardour of their convictions they depicted in glowing language the consequences of unrepented sin. Their enthusiasm and uncompromising devotion to their principles brought home to the awakening nation the horrors of the traffic in human flesh. Their very narrowness gave intensity and concentration to their work, the crowning glory of which was the passing of the Emancipation Bill, when the country paid twenty millions in cash to quiet the newly-awakened conscience, at the same time unconsciously throwing into the bargain the commercial prosperity of the West Indian colonies.

To return to Jamaica, we must not omit to mention that during the century we have been reviewing various dissenting bodies had sent out missionaries to Christianise the blacks. No churchman, however bigoted, would refuse to acknowledge the worth of their self-sacrificing and devoted labours, knowing well that much theological learning and zeal had been diverted from the Established Church on account of its unsympathetic attitude and inefficiency to cope with such ardent souls as the Wesleys and Whitfields of those days. Nor were the great Home Missionary Societies callous as to the religious condition of our plantations. The Church Missionary Society was in the field before that for the Propagation of the Gospel. Space forbids one to do more than to say that many men who were sent out died at their posts, doing their best, and making the way easier for those who followed. The first Bishop of Jamaica was Dr Lipscombe. He arrived in the island in 1824, a time when the agitation of anticipated emancipation was at its height, many of the planters threatening to transfer their allegiance to the United States, or even to assert their independence, for they foresaw the havoc which the measure would play with the sugar industry. Serious outbreaks occurred frequently amongst the blacks; lives were lost, property to the amount of £666,977 was destroyed on one occasion. In a statement of 1832 we find that during the eight years of the bishop's residence in the island thirteen churches had been built, nine were in course of erection. The diocese numbered forty-five clergy and thirty-two catechists, religious instruction being given on two hundred and eighty estates. At this time the Church was straggling hard to teach the liberated slaves how to use their freedom; and it is noteworthy that during the festivities with which the emancipation was celebrated, extending over three days, no riot, or trouble of any kind, is recorded.

It was during the episcopate of the second Bishop of Jamaica, Dr Spencer, that the Church Missionary Societies practically withdrew help from this colony. The S.P.G. missionary connection ceased in 1865, urging in explanation the more pressing needs of other mission-fields. In these years the Church suffered materially from the withdrawal of financial support. We read of closed chapels, dilapidated school-houses, scattered congregations; but there were more troublous days in store for it, and indeed for the whole island.

Successive floods and earthquakes half ruined the agricultural industries. Cholera carried away 32,000 souls, free trade had thrown half the sugar estates out of cultivation. Thus the depleted revenues of the colony, and the fact that nonconformist bodies were doing useful work without costing the State a halfpenny, whilst the Establishment cost the island treasury £37,284 a year, were considerations which induced the Jamaican Assembly to agree to measures of retrenchment, financially affecting the clergy, since it was evident that the State subsidies were, in view of the reduced revenues, utterly disproportionate.

Later in 1867 Sir J. P. Grant's first act was to direct the discontinuance from general revenue of all "charges for organists, beadles, and other church servants," which meant that congregations were in future to pay church expenses, which seems fair enough; but more ominous from a financial point of view was that Governor's statement that "no vacancy occurring in the ecclesiastical establishment would be filled up, until a new scheme for supplying the religious wants of the island should be determined on by Her Majesty's Government." Thus from 1866 until 1870 no new men replaced the vacancies left by those who died during those years. Here it is necessary to refer briefly to the risings at Morant Bay occasioned by the excited patriotism and fervid oratory of a man called Gordon, who inflamed the blacks by his democratic ravings. Froude says: "The crime for which he was arrested and hung was that he had dreamt of regenerating the negro race by baptising them in the Jordan of English Radicalism." Whether or not General Eyre was to be blamed in the prompt and vigorous measures he took for the protection of the island, at this time, may be open to question, but the direct consequence of his action was the surrender in 1865 of the old Legislative Assembly and the creation of the present Constitution, which is that of an ordinary Crown colony, of which Sir J. P. Grant was the first Governor.

It was about this time in England that Mr Gladstone introduced and carried his famous bill for the Disestablishment of the Irish Church. Under the impulse of that feeling, disestablishment and disendowment being in the air, the movement to place the colonial churches on the same footing as the Irish was suggested and proposed to most of the British dependencies. Some, like Demerara, disapproved of the proposals.

In the case of Jamaica from the standpoint of economic reform, apparently, there were good reasons for Disestablishment. Prior to 1825 all acts dealing with ecclesiastical affairs were permanent, but the clergy act of that date had definite terms of duration attached to it. Subsequent acts affecting the Church were also of a temporary character. At the Disestablishment in 1870 these durational clauses had lapsed. Six months after they had been in abeyance no attempt was made by the newly-constituted government to renew them, then the English Church in Jamaica knew it was disestablished.

In June 1870 a law was passed regulating the gradual disendowment of the Church of England in Jamaica. It also enabled Her late Majesty in due time to incorporate by charter the properly appointed representatives of the Church, after which incorporation the Governor had power to vest in that body all church property belonging to any rectory or curacy becoming vacant either by death or resignation, etc. It also secured the continuance of their stipends to those of the clergy who should continue in the due discharge of their ecclesiastical duties as members of the Voluntary Communion.

This year the thirty-fourth Synod was held according to Law 30 of 1870. In 1890 the results of its deliberations were summarised in a volume containing forty-five canons. I need scarcely refer to the times of commercial depression the West Indies have experienced to indicate the difficult and uphill work which lay before Bishop Courtenay and his successors in reorganising a recently disendowed and disestablished church, with State subsidies withdrawn, as well as grants from home societies. It was evident that if she were to exist at all the Church had only to look to herself for support. The question was, "To be or not to be?" Appeals to friends in England, however, met with liberal response. The laity in Jamaica came forward nobly at this juncture, and gave unstintedly their time, advice, and service; whilst heroic men in distant mountain huts and in isolated country mission-rooms, living on the merest pittance, devoted their lives to the work of the Church. The growing numbers, the increasing influence of the clergy, testify to her inherent vitality in no less degree than does the successful way in which she battled with a sea of troubles. Her Communion represents probably the largest number of worshippers, including the best educated people in the island.

To my mind, the history of the Church in Jamaica, during the last thirty years, is an object-lesson for a study on natural selection, and of that expression which applies so variously—the survival of the fittest. At the present day there are 109 churches, 122 licensed buildings and mission-rooms, 93 clergy licensed by the bishops, 115 honorary lay-readers, 165 catechists, and there are 261 church schools in the island earning from the Government £10,000 per annum.

No one can go through the length and breadth of the island as I have been, without being impressed by the fact that the life of a country parson out here is only to be lived by a man possessed with the missionary spirit. Poverty, isolation, bodily fatigue, and countless irritations are his lot. In towns it is better; but the long distances which churches and mission-stations lie apart in some districts means practically living on the roads. One lady, whose husband holds a country living, and who had come to Jamaica directly after her marriage, told me she had not spent £10 in the intervening six years on her own personal clothing. She was very happy notwithstanding, and amused me immensely by telling me that generally the loudest singer in church was invariably the Obeah man or woman in the district. One poor ecclesiastic, with a somewhat weak chin on an otherwise benevolent countenance, uttered the hardest criticism on Archbishop Nuttall I have heard since I have been in the island:

"The Archbishop," said he, in a tone of asperity, "was Kitchener in the Church." I laughed and said he "had Kitchenered to some purpose," but a semi-articulate growl came from a corner of the room, wishing there were a "few more Kitcheners about."

If in England we are inclined to associate Anglicanism in a setting of refined æstheticism, or with a scholastic environment, the Church of England in Jamaica, figuratively speaking, stares us in the face with its broad adaptability to the needs of semi-civilised negroes, as well as to those of the British settler. Its claim that we should sympathise with its aims, which in the face of discouraging and continued poverty it steadily pursues, in uplifting a once down-trodden and sinned-against race as well as in strengthening and supporting the more favoured, is one we must admit, if we possess a vestige of the spirit of justice.

A Wesleyan minister I met recently criticised the work of his Baptist brother in Jamaica as "shoddy." One can conscientiously maintain there is no shoddiness in the work of the Church of England in this island to-day.

True, its energies are cramped, its charitable works stunted for lack of funds, but the spirit of growth, expansion, and adaptability is latent within it, waiting only for the necessary means to press on towards its high calling.

To show the position of the Church of England from a numerical standpoint, in comparison with other religious bodies in 1865, at the time when Crown Government under Sir J. P. Grant superseded the old Legislative Assembly, I have copied a statistical table from the Rev J. P. Ellis' "Sketch of the History of the English Church in Jamaica," which shows that a little more than one quarter of the religious world in this colony belonged to the State-paid Church, supported as it was by £7,100 yearly from a British Government Consolidated Fund and £37,284 from the Inland Government.

	Accommodation.	Average Attendance.
Church of England	48,824	36,300
Wesleyan	41,775	37,570
Baptist	31,640	26,483
Presbyterian	12,575	7,955
Moravian	11,850	9,650
London Missionary Society	8,050	6,780
Roman Catholics	4,110	1,870
American Mission	1,550	775
Hebrew	1,000	500
Church of Scotland	1,000	450
TOTAL	192,374	128,333

The census of 1901 placed the population at 745,104. The number of registered church members is 33,000; and if in 1891, when Mr Ellis published his sketch, Archbishop Nuttall calculated the probable total number of persons actually, or nominally attached to the Church of England in Jamaica at 205,941, we may be sure that would, in 1903, be a considerable under-statement of the correct number benefited, or attending the ministrations of her churches. In 1879, when Bishop Courtenay retired from the see of Jamaica the staff of clergy numbered seventy-five, of whom forty-four were maintained by voluntary contributions. To-day there are ninety-three, all of whom are supported by the voluntary system, excepting three, who still receive payments from the old *régime* before 1865.

The income of the Church is now almost exclusively derived from the weekly collections and from the contributions of the registered members, the minimum fixed by the synod being three-pence a week. Each church sends all such monies thus collected to a central office at Kingston, from which they are administered.

I have already referred to the able manner in which His Grace, the Archbishop of the West Indies, has, since 1880, not only guided the Church of England in Jamaica through times of great depression, but has also expanded its activities, notwithstanding the changed state of its exchequer. Now that Jamaica's prosperous star is, we hope, once more in the ascendency, let us hope that those successful merchants whose money is got from its soil will not forget to treat their Church liberally and generously. Here I can but repeat what I have said on a previous page, one must have a personal acquaintance with the colonies, and the colonists themselves, to appreciate the way they look to Mother Church to supply their spiritual needs.

If I have digressed too much on these matters for the liking of some of my readers, let me appeal to that spirit of patriotic fraternity called imperialism which recent events in South Africa has set throbbing at the heart of English life, wherever the British flag flies, and ask them how they can fail to be concerned or interested in that which here represents the greatest good to the greatest number of King Edward's subjects.

If we are fascinated by the study of racial problems—and I confess my own liking for such books as Professor Tylor's "Primitive Culture" and W. S. Laing's "Human Origins"—our anthropological studies and ethnological leanings will lead us to perceive that that agency which has already, in so short a time, produced promising results out of such unpromising material in the raw, as the West African devil-worshipping black, claims our sympathy.

Finally, those to whom the "heavenly vision" is not a momentary and fleeting phantom, but an abiding reality, will not hesitate to extend by money and by influence, if they have either or both, the consolations of a Spiritual Kingdom to their less enlightened, or less privileged brethren in the British colonies and dependencies.

In connection with this great subject, I know no finer lines than those written by James Russell Lowell, the great American nature-loving poet. Believing that divinity, more or less, lies concealed in the commonplace garb of our humanity, he says:

> "Be noble! and the nobleness that lies
> In other men, sleeping, but never dead,
> Will rise in majesty to meet thine own."

CHAPTER XXI
SIR HENRY MORGAN—LORD RODNEY—EDUCATION IN JAMAICA—CAPTAIN BAKER ON THE BRIGHT PROSPECTS OF JAMAICA

If Jamaica was known as the white man's grave in a bygone age, it has now completely changed its character. Twenty-five years ago Chief-Justice Cockburn declared that "there was not a stone in the island of Jamaica which, if the rains of heaven had not washed off from it the stains of blood, might not have borne terrible witness to the manner in which martial law had been exercised for the suppression of native discontent."

I was told only yesterday of the panic-stricken way in which the natives learnt of the death of the late Queen Victoria. A nonconformist minister, whose sphere of work lies amongst the mountains at the eastern end of the island, graphically described to me how the inhabitants of those isolated parts flocked into the nearest towns and to the parsonage houses, chattering anxiously together about the death of the great "Missus Queen." Some native agitators had worked upon their ignorance and credulity, and they quite believed with the accession "of the new young man" slavery times would come again!

In the place of native discontent it would, at the present day, be difficult to find a more loyal, peaceful, and law-abiding people than this. And yet it is not more than two hundred and fifty years since the wildest of buccaneers figured upon the scene in Jamaica. In a biographical dictionary I note the somewhat amusing, though deeply satirical piece of information.

"Morgan, Sir Henry John, buccaneer, born about 1637, long ravaged the Spanish colonies, took and plundered Puerto Bello 1668; *after a life of rapine knighted by Charles II.* and made a marine commissary, died 1690."

This great freebooter was as politic and shrewd as he was unscrupulous and daring. I cannot vouch for the truth of the following story, but it is characteristic of those days.

When summoned to England to answer for his piratical excursion on the Spanish Main, he offered King Charles such magnificent pearls for the adornment of his favourite ladies, that any thought of punishment was immediately banished from the royal brain. Instead, Sir Henry Morgan returned loaded with honours to the West Indies.

But I would like to relate how, by a brilliant stratagem, he extricated his ships from a position of great danger. In 1654, Maracaibo had been sacked by L'Olonnais, another notorious freebooter, but in 1668 it had regained its former reputation as one of the richest towns of Spanish America, and Morgan determined to attack it. Like Santiago in Cuba, it lay on the shores of a long bay with so narrow a mouth that almost one ship was sufficient to block it. Morgan entered the bay with three ships, stormed the town and took the fort. It seems that his victorious companions were celebrating their success with wine in the fort, left by their late enemies, when their indefatigable and valiant captain stepped outside to see how matters stood. All was silent, but Morgan despatched one hundred men into the woods to hunt up the late inhabitants, who had betaken themselves thither with their money and treasure. They returned with thirty prisoners, who were inhumanly tortured, to disclose the hiding-places of their wealth.

The Inquisition had taught the English mariners of those days how to rack and how to burn. When Morgan, after some thirty days of this cruelty, finally sailed away, to his consternation he found the mouth of the harbour blocked by three Spanish men-of-war, the crews of which had also rebuilt the fort at the entrance of the harbour. Full of resource, Morgan coolly ordered the plunder and prisoners to be removed from his largest vessel to the smaller ships. He filled the former instead with gunpowder, pitch, tar, and combustibles. He mounted wooden cannon upon the vessel and dressed up posts to resemble men. Having completed his preparations, he sent word to the commander of the Spanish warships saying, unless a heavy ransom was paid, he would burn Maracaibo to the ground. The reply of the Spanish Admiral was to the effect that unless Morgan surrendered in three days he would pay the ransom in lead. At this crisis the great freebooter next morning sailed in single file down the harbour, the dummy ship leading, in charge of some daring men, who, at a signal from their intrepid chief, were to light the fuses and escape in a small boat to the other ships.

When the Spanish Admiral thus saw Morgan's first and largest vessel heading directly for him, he sailed into the harbour to meet him, grappling and making fast his ship to that of his enemy, expecting to fight hand-to-hand. Just at this moment the matches were applied, and in the noise and confusion the Spanish ship could not unfasten sufficiently quickly the grappling chains and irons which fastened the two ships together in a deadly embrace.

The consequence was that it caught fire, and, in a few minutes, both were blazing from stem to stern.

Rather than fall into the hands of the buccaneers, the Spaniards jumped overboard. The crews of the two remaining ships ran them aground, and rushed to the woods to hide themselves. However, the fort further down had yet to be passed, but Morgan executed a manœuvre which so alarmed the garrison, who expected an attack in the rear, that they removed their cannon some distance from the fort. When this was done, Morgan sailed away out of the harbour, his crews jeering at the Spanish garrison, who were unable to bring their ordnance back in time to fire on the bold and resourceful pirate.

Passing on to events which took place in Caribbean waters over a hundred years later, one's heart swells with pride when one remembers how Lord Rodney, of glorious memory, whose statue adorns Spanish Town, saved not only Jamaica, but our other West Indian possessions in 1782, upholding the honour of the nation at a most critical time in English history. The American colonies were lost. France, Spain, and Holland, our ocean rivals, had united to make one great effort to wrest from us our naval superiority. At home, Irish patriots clamoured then, as now, for what they conceived to be their rights.

Lord Rodney, who had taken the Leeward Islands from France, commanded in the West Indies. He had already punished the Dutch for taking part in the alliance by capturing the island of Eustachius and three millions' worth of stores and money. Burke, whose policy somewhat resembled that of the little Englanders of these days, notwithstanding his successes, had him called home to account for his actions. In his absence the French fleet recaptured the Leeward Islands and Eustachius, and thereby became the paramount power in these seas. Things became so desperate that Rodney was immediately sent back to his post. After a mid-winter cruise of five stormy weeks he came upon the combined fleets off the mountainous coasts of Dominica. In number of ships the fleets were about equal, but in size and men the French were vastly superior, having 14,000 soldiers on board besides the ships' full complement, destined for "the conquest of Jamaica."

For two days the rival fleets manœuvred opposite each other, but during the night of the 11th of April 1872, Rodney signalled to the fleet to sail southwards. The French thought he was flying. Instead, he tacked at 2 A.M. on the next day. At dawn the French were on his lee quarter. At 7 A.M. the British fleet, Rodney leading in the *Formidable*, sailing in an oblique direction, cut the French line, thus throwing the ships into confusion. They were unable to reform. The conflict resolved itself into a series of separate contests. The cannons roared all day, the French ships one by one either foundered, or hauled down their flag. The *Ville de Paris*, De Grasses' flagship, and the pride of the French navy, was the last to yield. The slaughter had been frightful, 14,000 are said to have been killed, besides prisoners. One half of the fleet was taken, or sunk; the rest of the ships, like the Spanish galleons after the Armada, staggered away to hide their wounds and humiliation.

Had Rodney received the hasty instructions a timorous-hearted Government despatched to him before this engagement, which were: "Strike your flag and come home," the history of Jamaica would be a very different thing to-day.

On that ever memorable occasion the combined strength of France, Spain and Holland failed to wrest from Britannia her sovereignty of the seas. The laurels with which the heroes of Elizabethan days had crowned her still rested on her brow. Though sorely smitten, she could still hold aloft in untarnished glory the sceptre of ocean rule.

It is hard to tear one's thoughts away from the glorious scenes where the history of the great British race has been made. I cannot, however, draw my remarks to a close on the West Indies without referring to another way in which we add to the glory and stability of the Empire to which we are proud to belong. I am alluding to the education which in Jamaica is provided by government for the younger generation of this colony.

By a law passed in 1890, all elementary schools must be undenominational, that is, if they are to be recognised by the Government, and special attention is to be directed to agriculture and manual training both in training and elementary schools. At this date, schools deemed unnecessary were closed, others were amalgamated to render efficiency and economy more practical. In 1900, 757 elementary schools, including infant schools, received grants from Government. Children from six to fourteen years attend. Grants are given according to marks gained at examinations and on average attendances. Subjects for examinations include, besides organisation and discipline, reading, recitation, writing, English, and arithmetic, also elementary science, the secondary subjects being morals, Scripture, drawing, manual occupation, geography and singing. Schools on the Annual Grant List are examined by special standards. A registered teacher gets in a school of 150 children £30; if certificated £36.

Forty male students are supported by Government at the Mico training college to be trained as school-masters.

At Shortwood, in the parish of St Andrew, thirty girls are trained to be school-mistresses, also at the expense of the Government, which pays the manager of certain voluntary training colleges

£25 a year each, for a specified number of resident students under training.

The Mico College is one of the handsomest buildings in Kingston. Jane, Lady Mico, widow of Sir Samuel Mico, a city knight, and member of the Mercers' Company, died in 1666, and bequeathed £1000 "to redeem poor slaves." This sum, invested by the Court of Chancery in London property, grew to the large amount of £120,000, when, in 1834, Sir T. F. Buxton thought the interest might very properly be applied to educating West Indian children. Of several schools in the West Indies established for this purpose, the only one remaining is the Mico College of Jamaica. The Government of the island is also very liberal in the way of offering scholarships, the best of which is one for £200 tenable three years, granted to a candidate who shall have passed in Honour Lists in the Cambridge Senior Examination, and who shall fulfil the rest of the conditions attached to it.

There is a Theological College in Kingston, where students are trained for holy orders: a very necessary institution, for about one-third of the island clergy represent the coloured and black element of the population.

Another very useful and charitable institution in Kingston is the Deaconess Home, where the education is specially intended for the coloured children of a class superior to those who attend the elementary schools, and who are not *gratae personae* at the ladies' schools in Kingston. This is really a work which is much needed, since it is unpractical to educate coloured men to fill responsible posts, if an equivalent effort is not made with the girls of the same class to render them companionable and helpful as wives. Nurses are trained in this Home, and all good works, such as temperance meetings, are undertaken. I was present myself at a service held by the Sisters, exclusively for the sailors who come to this port of Kingston. It did one good to see how at home these poor fellows seemed with the kindly women who addressed them. Each asked for his favourite hymn to be sung, and they were in no hurry to quit at the close of the proceedings. At a temperance meeting, held a few days afterwards, I was present when eight of them signed the pledge. Unfortunately, this good work is direfully in need of funds.

In conclusion, I cannot do better than give the gist of an article in which the bright future of Jamaica is looked forward to confidently, by one who must know, far better than myself, the financial attitude of the country. The writer is Captain L. D. Baker, a Bostonian, the head of the United Fruit Company, to whom, in company with Sir Alfred Jones of the Elder Dempster line, Jamaica owes much of its recent return to comparative prosperity. He says to those wanting to invest: "Investments in this country are safe, if in land for agricultural purposes. Values are normal; titles are as good and as well protected as any in the world. Our Governors have been the best that Britain can give to her colonies. By them we enjoy guaranteed safety and success."

Speaking of the advance Jamaica has made since the days of Governor Darling, 1868, Captain Baker reviews the benefits the island has derived from each successive governor; he says: "To Sir J. P. Grant we owe the irrigation of the parched lands of the Spanish Town district. He turned them into a fertile plain. We next had Sir Anthony Musgrave. He gave the telegraph, and he gave steamship lines and railway extensions and general enterprise such an impetus that they have not ceased," etc. Next came Sir Henry Norman, whose "steady brain kept the enthusiastic and the erratic man in check, so that there should be no regrets." After him came Sir Henry Blake, and the writer of this article cannot praise that popular Governor too highly: "Ever full of indomitable enterprise and push—exhibitions, hotels, agricultural societies, agricultural schemes, willingly launching out his own money, riding through the country hither and thither, stirring up everyone that had a bit of enterprise in his nature. He left us, throwing his burden at the feet of Mr Chamberlain, to be taken up by him." The present Governor, Sir A. Hemming, took up the work with equal zest and push. He presented the situation to his "double steam-engine friend, Sir Alfred Jones, thereby inaugurating the direct line, and consummating what may be justly termed a grand success for the future of the island." It is good reading to hear this successful American business man say that neither he "nor his companies know anything but kindness from this Government."

Jamaica is one of our oldest colonies; she has been rich, but now is poor; still, with patience, prosperity will revisit her shores. What one can say best to one's country people is, Come and make her acquaintance; the beauty of the scenery will repay you for your trouble. Her associations with the past will kindle your sympathy and evoke your interest.

www.ingramcontent.com/pod-product-compliance
Lightning Source LLC
Chambersburg PA
CBHW061257110426
42742CB00012BA/1951